SEXUALITY IN VICTORIAN FICTION

Oklahoma Project for
Discourse and Theory

OKLAHOMA PROJECT FOR DISCOURSE AND THEORY

SERIES EDITORS

Robert Con Davis, University of Oklahoma
Ronald Schleifer, University of Oklahoma

ADVISORY BOARD

SEXUALITY IN VICTORIAN FICTION

By Dennis W. Allen

University of Oklahoma Press
Norman and London

Chapter 2, "No Love for Lydia: The Fate of Desire in *Pride and Prejudice*," is a revised version of an article that first appeared in *TSLL* 27, no. 4 (1985): 425–43.

Allen, Dennis W. (Dennis Winslow), 1951–
    Sexuality in Victorian fiction / by Dennis W. Allen.
        p.   cm. — (Oklahoma project for discourse and theory ; v. 15)
    Includes bibliographical references and index.
    ISBN 0-8061-2547-0 (alk. paper)
        1. English fiction—19th century—History and criticism. 2. Sex
in literature. 3. Erotic stories, English—History and criticism.
4. Psychoanalysis and literature. 5. Body, Human, in literature.
I. Title. II. Series.
PR878.S49A43   1993   93-16225
823'.8093538—dc20   CIP

Sexuality in Victorian Fiction is Volume 15 of the Oklahoma Project for Discourse and Theory.

The paper in this book meets the guidelines for permanence and durability of the Committee on Production Guidelines for Book Longevity of the Council on Library Resources, Inc. ∞

1   2   3   4   5   6   7   8   9   10

For my parents

Contents

Series Editors' Foreword

The Oklahoma Project for Discourse & Theory is a series of interdisciplinary texts whose purpose is to explore the cultural institutions that constitute the human sciences, to see them in relation to one another, and, perhaps above all, to see them as products of particular discursive practices. To this end, we hope that the Oklahoma Project will promote dialogue within and across traditional disciplines—psychology, philology, linguistics, history, art history, aesthetics, logic, political economy, religion, philosophy, anthropology, communications, and the like—in texts that theoretically are located across disciplines. In recent years, in a host of new and traditional areas, there has been great interest in such discursive and theoretical frameworks. Yet we conceive of the Oklahoma Project as going beyond local inquiries, providing a larger forum for interdiscursive theoretical discussions and dialogue.

Our agenda in previous books and certainly in this one has been to present through the University of Oklahoma Press a series of critical volumes that set up a theoretical encounter among disciplines, an interchange not limited to literature but covering virtually the whole range of the human sciences. It is a critical series with an important reference in literary studies—thus mirroring the modern development of discourse theory—but including all approaches, other than quantitative studies, open to semiotic and post-semiotic analysis and to the wider concerns of cultural studies. Regardless of its particular domain, each book in the series will investigate characteristically post-Freudian, post-Saussurean, and post-Marxist questions about culture and the discourses that constitute different cultural phenomena. The Oklahoma Project is a sustained dialogue intended to make a significant contribution to the contemporary understanding of the human sciences in the contexts of cultural theory and cultural studies.

The title of the series reflects, of course, its home base, the University of Oklahoma. But it also signals in a significant way the particularity of the *local* functions within historical and conceptual frameworks for understanding culture. *Oklahoma* is a haunting place-name in American culture. A Choctaw phrase meaning "red people," it goes back to the Treaty of Dancing Rabbit Creek in Mississippi in 1830. For Franz Kafka, it conjured up the idea of America itself, both the indigenous Indian peoples of North America and the vertiginous space of the vast plains. It is also the place-name, the "American" starting point, with which Wallace Stevens begins his *Collected Poems*. Historically, too, it is a place in which American territorial and political expansion was reenacted in a single day in a retracing called the Oklahoma land run. Geographically, it is the heartland of the continent.

As such—in the interdisciplinary Oklahoma Project for Discourse & Theory—we are hoping to describe, above all, multifaceted *interests* within and across various studies of discourse and culture. Such interests are akin to what Kierkegaard calls the "in-between" aspect of experience, the "inter esse," and, perhaps more pertinently, what Nietzsche describes as the always *political* functioning of concepts, art works, and language—the functioning of power as well as knowledge in discourse and theory. Such politics, occasioning dialogue and bringing together powerfully struggling and often unarticulated positions, disciplines, and assumptions, is always local, always particular. In some ways, such interests function in broad feminist critiques of language, theory, and culture as well as microphilosophical and microhistorical critiques of the definitions of truth and art existing within ideologies of "disinterested" meaning. They function in the interested examination of particular disciplines and general disciplinary histories. They function (to allude to two of our early titles) in the very interests of theory and the particularity of the postmodern age in which many of us find ourselves. In such interested particulars, we believe, the human sciences are articulated. We hope that the books of the Oklahoma Project will provide sites of such interest and that in them, individually and collectively, the monologues of traditional scholarly discourse will become heteroglosses, just as such place-names as *Oklahoma* and such commonplace words and concepts as *discourse* and *theory* can become sites for the dialogue and play of culture.

ROBERT CON DAVIS
RONALD SCHLEIFER

Norman, Oklahoma

Preface

This study was generated by some of the implications of Michel Foucault's rejection of the "repressive hypothesis," namely, the notion that the Victorians simply and unilaterally refused to consider the sexual. On the contrary, Foucault argues, the proliferation of scientific and social discourses on sex and sexuality during the Victorian era demonstrates a vast enterprise designed to articulate—in effect to produce—the "truth" of the sexual. Although Foucault argues that we can no longer consider the Victorians as "Victorian," as impossibly prudish in the popular sense of the term, he does not claim that public discourse on sexuality in the nineteenth century was as explicit as in our own time. Foucault's analysis thus radically complicates our understanding of the representation of sex and sexuality in Victorian fiction. Erotically discreet, the Victorian novel nonetheless subtly constructs the sexual. As such, the erotic discretion of Victorian fiction cannot be seen simply as an unproblematic instance of sexual prudery. Rather, it is precisely this sexual discretion that needs to be explained, situated in a larger context of cultural and social forces.

My thesis is that the erotic reserve of the Victorian novel is a complex reflection of the difficulty of reconciling nineteenth-century constructions of sex and sexuality with the larger ideological framework of the culture, a response to the contemporary perception that sex and sexuality threaten to disrupt the social order and the self. Moreover, I argue that the difficulty of representing the sexual is not a uniquely Victorian problem, for the nineteenth-century sense of the sexual as anarchic reflects the actual inef-

xiii

fability of the sexual, the tendency of sex and sexuality to resist and disrupt attempts to represent them. In the last analysis, Victorian representations of the sexual are also an effort to define, and hence control, sex and sexuality.

It is probably already apparent that, as an attempt to analyze the sexual field as the Victorians constituted it, this book draws its methodology from recent historicized work in cultural studies. As the latter part of my thesis implies, however, I have also incorporated insights from psychoanalysis, both Freudian and Lacanian, into this study. In a sense this blend of approaches is an unusual one. Yet the combination of a historicized approach with some of the inherently ahistorical assertions of psychoanalysis about sex and sexuality is not, I think, as contradictory as it first appears. To begin with, most of the psychoanalytic material used here is itself read historically. Thus I situate Freudian theory in its cultural context, seeing it as both the culmination and the overt articulation of Victorian conceptions of the sexual. Such an enterprise is actually aided by the work of Lacan and Leo Bersani, whose view of the psychic as an arena of language and the symbolic—of psychoanalysis as precisely the study of representations—allows for the historicized reading of such representations.

Thus, if historical and psychoanalytic ("ahistorical") ways of discussing literature often strike us as incompatible, the reason probably lies less in any inherent impossibility of combining the insights derived from these approaches than in a related conflict. The current debate between constructionist and essentialist readings of "human nature" would seem to posit a clear opposition between two conceptions of the categories of "human experience": as products of temporally and spatially localized cultural forces *or* as timeless and universal "realities." Generally, this study sides with the former position, seeing sex and sexuality as cultural constructs that are differently constituted in different cultural settings. By extension, I read Victorian perceptions of a number of related concepts, from the body to gender to identity to sexual preference, as perceptions, whose significance lies in their reflection, not of a transcendental "reality," but of Victorian cultural beliefs.

Because it specifies a "nature" for the sexual, however, if only as inherently disruptive of attempts to represent it, this work is, in a crucial sense, founded on a certain essentialism. I designate an "essence" for the sexual here advisedly and for a number of reasons. The first is that such a conception of sex and sexuality (as intrinsically resistant to textualization) seems to match Victorian perceptions of and anxieties about the sexual, articulating a certain pressure that underlies the novels examined here. In and of itself, such a perception could simply be examined as part of the Victorian construction of the sexual field. I have chosen, however, to situate the "nature" of the sexual outside of this historical context for two additional reasons.

The first is a question of honesty. As Diana Fuss demonstrates in *Essentially Speaking* (1989), the binary opposition in contemporary criticism between constructionism and essentialism is always illusory, with essentialist constructs inhabiting even the purest of constructionist arguments. As such, my articulation of the sexual as ineffable is, as Fuss would surely note, essentialist, a reification of sex and sexuality—if only as a locus of undecidability. This reification is not intended, however, to "remystify" the sexual or to forestall intellectual inquiry but rather to foreground what would otherwise remain hidden: the fact that, as a set of related epistemological categories, sex and sexuality are already reified, their very constitution as objects of study presupposing the transhistorical, even transcendental, reality of such categories. By directly specifying an "essence" for the sexual, I openly acknowledge this difficulty.

Moreover, if a certain essentialism is apparently unavoidable, even in attempts to disassemble the hegemonic constructs of Western thought, Fuss persuasively argues that essentialism per se is not inherently reactionary, an inevitable reinforcement of the hegemonic. Rather, its impact depends on how it is deployed. As such, the final reason for my definition of the sexual as disruptive, as resistant to narrativization, is that it strikes me as the most politically useful way of constituting "sex" and "sexuality," articulating a definition that simultaneously acknowledges the apparent inescapability of such categories while at the same time virtually voiding those categories of a definitive content. Such a strategy, I hope, both allows a basis for the discussion that follows and, at the same time, prevents or forestalls any easy projection back onto the Victorians of contemporary understandings of the "meanings" of such terms. As a result, the sexual can be turned back on itself, not only allowing the examination of how it was constituted by the

Victorians, but implicitly interrogating our own constructions of the sexual field.

By the same token, the selection of novels that I have chosen to analyze here says, perhaps, as much about contemporary critical concerns as it does about the attempts of various Victorian novelists both to produce and to contain sex and sexuality. In the first place, my choice of works by Austen, Gaskell, Dickens, and Wilde was animated, in part, by the desire to strike a balance between female and male authors and between canonically "major" novels *(Pride and Prejudice, Bleak House)* and works that have traditionally been considered "minor" *(Cranford, The Picture of Dorian Gray).* Moreover, I have tried to select novels that intersect with and illuminate each other in a variety of ways. As a result, the choice of these texts could be said to constitute a certain narrative, or rather narratives, about Victorian representations of sex and sexuality.

Thus the novels by Austen and Wilde, written at the beginning and the end of the century, are intended not only to provide some rough temporal perimeters for this project but also to mark the constitution and deconstruction of a particular literary mode of representing sex and sexuality. Because this mode is inextricably linked to contemporary notions of the bourgeois subject, to a "depth model" of subjectivity, this study could be said to tell the story of the production (and, finally, the rejection) of "repression," of the idea of a hidden (sexual) secret as the "meaning" of both individuals and texts. In addition to this temporal narrative, I also present a "rhetorical" story, showing how Gaskell and Dickens struggle with the implications of the representational codes of narrative discretion outlined by Austen, specifically with the difficulties of articulating the "nature" of "gender" or "identity," given the erasure of the body from nineteenth-century fiction. Read in this context, Wilde's novel both demonstrates the failure of Victorian narrative discretion and inaugurates an alternate representational mode.

Moreover, I have chosen works that problematize issues closely related to Victorian (and contemporary) conceptions of sexuality: novels that both illustrate and question nineteenth-century constructions of the body, gender, sexual preference, and identity. This narrative, which could be called political, demonstrates the complex relation of the individual authors to the sexual ideology of Victorian culture. If these works were shaped by the cultural field in which they were produced, they also, as literary productions by middle-class writers, were part of the articulation of that very field. As such, the relation of each of these writers to Victorian sexual ideology is a complex one. All of the authors examined here were enfranchised by the dominant culture (if only by virtue of their social class and the legitimacy conferred by publication), and all of these novels served to reinforce the dominant (bourgeois) ideology of Victorian culture. Each of these writers, however, was (or felt) in some way marginalized within that culture (by virtue of gender or sexual preference or, in the case of Dickens, by anxiety about downward social mobility). As such, while the novels I examine are read as working to constitute and reinforce the hegemonic Victorian sexual ideology outlined in chapter 1, yet I have also tried to call attention to points of resistance in each text, places where the writer negotiates with or tries to revise the dominant system of beliefs. As a narrative of (ideological) containment and resistance, then, this study must be read not as an agon of reified concepts ("the author" versus "society") but as the more complex story of the competing impulses of ideological cooperation and refusal *within* each author.

Finally, despite the organization of this study through the temporal, rhetorical, and political narratives constituted by the selection of these authors and works, such stories are not intended as "master narratives," as *the* statements of what "sex" and "sexuality" were for the Victorians. Nor is this book designed as an exhaustive survey of strategies for representing the sexual in Victorian fiction. While these novels are typical or representative, their treatments of the sexual should not be seen as definitive. As is the case with any study of this sort, a different selection of texts would have told a slightly different story or stories, and the intention of this project is to suggest some of the principles animating Victorian configurations of the sexual field rather than to provide a fixed (and hence false) definition of that field.

Chapter 1 outlines the thesis of this study, and provides its historical background, examining the Victorian perceptions of sex and sexuality that frame these works. Using a variety of texts, from travel writing to Freud, from Darwin to Mayhew, I argue that the erotic discretion of Victorian fiction derives from a complicated sense of the sexual as chaotic, not only because it was seen as outside of the "order" of civilization, but also because of its potential to call into question the binary oppositions (between, for example, the civilized and the savage) and the taxonomies (such as the class system) that defined the text of Victorian culture. In other words, sex for the Victorians was both chaotic and "in-different," antithetical to the production of difference. As such, the sexual was perceived by the Victorians as alien to the general principles of binarism and taxonomy that organized their universe. Finally, I argue that the sexual discretion of Victorian literature reflects a difficulty of meaning, a sense that the sexual resists representation. As such, the Victorian novels examined here can be seen as projects for the management of sex and sexuality that attempt to define its ineffability and to suggest modes for restraining its potential for the disruption of the self, the social order, or the conceptual foundations of Victorian culture.

Chapter 2 looks at Jane Austen's *Pride and Prejudice,* which serves as something of a pre-text for the analyses that follow it. Literally written before the Victorian era, the work indicates the basic principles governing the erotic reticence of the Victorian novel. Focusing primarily on sexual desire, perhaps the most uncontrollable aspect of sexuality, Austen implicitly associates the sexual with disorder and the erasure of cultural distinctions. Her response is to construct a doctrine of sexual "repression" that serves to redefine sexual desire in a socially acceptable form and allows her to develop a variety of narrative techniques for articulating the sexual, for producing and defining as well as controlling it.

Coming at midcentury, Elizabeth Gaskell's *Cranford* and Charles Dickens's *Bleak House* exemplify the progressive complexity of the treatment of sexuality in the Victorian era. In these novels, we can track the gradual shift in emphasis from a concern with the social impact of the sexual to anxiety about its destabilizing effect on the self, a shift that becomes apparent in Gaskell and is fully realized in Dickens. Moreover, both novels illustrate how the difficulties of representing sexuality induce related conceptual problems. Because the repression of the sexual usually involves or implies the repression of the body, sexual reticence in Victorian fiction creates an extended crisis of representation, problematizing such ideas as "gender" (in Gaskell's case) and "identity" (in Dickens's), ideas implicitly based on and articulated through the body. The strategies employed by these novelists to resolve such difficulties demonstrate an increasing sophistication, with Gaskell reworking cultural fictions of gender difference to mediate between the competing demands of "biology" and "decorum," and Dickens manipulating the nature of representation itself. Finally, although this study does not pretend to explore fully the gendering of sexuality and desire in Victorian culture or fiction, the chapters on Gaskell and Dickens are intended to adumbrate contrasting female and male perspectives on the sexual.

Written at the end of the century, during the period when the construction of a recognizable notion of homosexuality reorganized the sexual field, Oscar Wilde's *Picture of Dorian Gray* both summarizes and extends the reasons for Victorian sexual anxiety. Focusing, like Austen, on sexual desire, Wilde is concerned with a newly articulated "homosexual" eros onto which are projected all the antitaxonomic and destabilizing properties attributed to sexuality in general. As a result, the work not only portrays the consequent dissolution of the characters' identities but finally enacts the effects of sexuality in the disintegration of the narrative itself. As such, Wilde's novel recapitulates the reasons for sexual anxiety in Victorian fiction, the threats it poses not only to the social structure or individual identity but to the novel itself. Both the epitome and the logical conclusion of Victorian struggles with the representation of the sexual, Wilde's novel finally also looks ahead, foreshadowing a radically different, modern response to the "imperfect pleasures" of sex and sexuality.

Acknowledgments

This book could not have been written without the generous assistance of a number of people. Sophia Blaydes, Terry Castle, and Beth Daniell provided invaluable criticism of the initial drafts of the manuscript. Carmen Cavallo and Richard Isomaki were equally helpful in their assessments of later versions. Hayden Ward, an inexhaustible source of information on the Victorians, provided valuable suggestions throughout. I would particularly like to thank Pat O'Donnell, Tim Sweet, and Cheryl Torsney for their careful attention to the manuscript in all of its many incarnations.

Work on this book was also vastly aided by the support and encouragement of numerous friends and colleagues. I am especially grateful to Tim Adams, Laura Brady, Sally Raines Brown, Anna Elfenbein, Elaine Ginsberg, Donald Hall, Jenny Jones, Jean Kempf, John Lamb, Darrin McNeice, Jean-Paul Pichardie, Scott Pitman, Jim Reid, Andrea Soccorsi, Sharon Stein, Gregg Thumm, Jack Torsney, Françoise Vidal, Tony Whitmore, and Raymond and Michéle Willems. Last but not least, without Michele Spitznogle's editorial assistance and unfailing good humor, this book would not have been possible.

Finally, institutional support was crucial at the inception of the project. Initial research was done as part of a Fulbright Lectureship in France, and early drafts of the Introduction and the Austen chapter were produced under the auspices of two West Virginia University Faculty Senate Grants. A radically different version of the Austen chapter was originally published in *Texas Studies in Literature and Language;* I thank the editors for permission to reprint sections of that essay here.

SEXUALITY IN
VICTORIAN FICTION

CHAPTER I

Introduction

At first glance, Thomas Hardy's *Tess of the d'Urbervilles* would seem to confirm the traditional view of one of the limits of the nineteenth-century English novel: an inability to deal frankly with sex, a prudish refusal to confront sexual activity or desire. Most noticeably, the scene of Tess's ruin at the hands of Alec d'Urberville is excessively reticent by modern standards. Having left Tess in the woods at night, Alec returns to find her asleep: "He knelt and bent lower, till her breath warmed his face, and in a moment his cheek was in contact with hers. She was sleeping soundly, and upon her eyelashes there lingered tears" ([1891] 1978, 119). What follows, at least in terms of narrative action, is—nothing. Description ceases, to be replaced by philosophical speculation. Where, the narrator wonders, is Tess's guardian angel? Why has she been "doomed" to such a fate? Concluding his discussion with the discreet statement that "an immeasurable social chasm" will now divide Tess's personality from her "previous self," Hardy ends not only the chapter but the first section of the novel. When the narrative resumes, the time is several weeks later, and the reader is left to infer what happened to Tess that night in the woods. Even in the 1890s, in a climate of greater sexual frankness than had obtained during most of the century, Hardy refuses to narrate Tess's fall, and this silence confirms our sense of the anxiety the Victorians felt about the expression of sexuality, about sexuality itself.

The novel as a whole, however, demonstrates that matters are more complicated than this. For one thing, silence is not an abso-

3

lute, an inevitable eradication of what is not mentioned. Depending on the context, it can reveal as well as conceal, its very presence acting as a coded form of disclosure. The narrator's discreet elision of the rape of Tess is itself evidence of that rape because a more innocent event would not have been shrouded in secrecy. Nor can the novel really be said to ignore sexuality, if only because Tess's fall provides the core of the book, the central incident that controls and shapes the entire narrative. In fact, upon closer inspection, sexuality permeates *Tess*. Precisely because Tess's loss of virginity is not directly narrated, the (absent) scene occurs over and over again, symbolically encoded in every event and accident that lead up to it. Thus the death of the horse that induces Tess's parents to send her to the d'Urbervilles for help is caused by a wound from a cart shaft "like a sword" that causes a flow of blood, splashing Tess "from face to skirt" with "crimson drops." A similar flow occurs as an "ill omen" when Tess, returning from her first meeting with Alec, pricks herself on a thorn of the rose he has placed in the bosom of her dress. Even the broken jar of molasses, which precipitates the quarrel with Car Darch that causes Tess to ride off with Alec into the woods, combines the imagery of the fluid and the phallic, the "black stream" of treacle glistening "like a slimy snake" in the moonlight. Instead of relentlessly excluding the sexual, Hardy would seem to embrace it, sexualizing all of reality.

As *Tess* suggests, the Victorian novel is neither hopelessly prudish nor resolutely frank.[1] Sexually discreet, Hardy's narrative also produces the erotic, both avoids and approaches the sexual. But why this curious dual movement? To answer the question, we must focus, like the Victorians themselves, on sexual reticence. Why, then, does Hardy center his novel on a sexual event that cannot itself be narrated? At first glance, the answer is obvious. Hardy's discretion is simply a response to contemporary demands for a literature that does not offend moral sensibilities by flaunting the sexual. To answer the question in this way, however, is simply to re-pose it. Why did the Victorians require a literature of erotic discretion? Such discretion is usually seen as the result of contemporary religious trends, but, I will argue, the sexual circumspection of Victorian novelists is generated by more complex and far-reaching pressures than the impact of Evangelical Christianity.[2] To begin with, the erotic reserve of the Victorian novel

4

reflects the difficulty of inserting Victorian ideas of sex and sexuality into the larger ideological framework of nineteenth-century English culture. Perceived as chaotic, the sexual is seen as a threat not only to particular instances of Victorian ideology (such as belief in the opposition of culture and nature or in the class system) but also to the very conceptual structures—binary oppositions, taxonomy—on which such beliefs, and Victorian society itself, are predicated. Moreover, the difficulty of representing the sexual is not, finally, a uniquely Victorian problem. Ultimately, Victorian conceptions of sex and sexuality as anarchic reflect the actual ineffability of the sexual, the tendency of sex and sexuality to resist and disrupt *any* attempt to represent them.

DEFINITIONS

To understand the difficulties posed by the representation of the sexual in the Victorian novel, we must first define such troublesome terms as *sex* and *sexuality*. As Michel Foucault has pointed out, however, it is precisely the idea of definition that is the problem, for the sexual is not a realm of meanings that we discover but rather a complex of ideas that we create. According to Foucault, the history of sexuality since the seventeenth century has been primarily an attempt by cultural institutions such as the medical establishment to define and control sexuality. This "something called 'sexuality,'" however, which is supposed to embody the "truth of sex and its pleasures," is not really a representation of a furtive reality that scientific discourses uncover; rather, it is a construct of those very discourses. Constituted as a "field of meanings to decipher," as the locus of hidden operations and subtle causal processes, "sexuality" is actually a formulation of the assumptions implicit in the techniques and methods used to "investigate" it (Foucault 1978, 68–69, 105–6).

If "sexuality" is merely a cultural construct, what then is the reality on which the idea of sexuality is based? If "sexuality" is taken to mean sexual desires and behaviors, the answer would seem to be "sex"—the biological forces, properties, and pleasures that serve as the basis for sexual activity. But "sex" too is a cultural fiction, an "artificial unity" of sensations, anatomical elements, and biological functions, and this unity is the most subtle element in what Foucault has called the "deployment of sexuality," the construction of sexuality as an area of knowledge and scientific study by Western culture. Presented as the causal principle, the reality, behind sexuality, "sex" has been advanced as "an omnipresent meaning . . . and as a universal signified," as the latent truth of our sexual desires and identities. "Sex," however, is finally a questionable gestalt (Foucault 1978, 154). As with sexuality, the meaning of sex, the notion of sex as meaning, is entirely a creation of cultural discourses.

There would seem to be, then, no real foundation for our notions of sexuality or sex. For Foucault, the physical basis for these concepts is simply the body, the site of sensations and biological processes. As Thomas Laqueur has demonstrated, however, the body too "is so hopelessly bound to its cultural meanings as to elude unmediated access" (1990, 12). Laqueur is particularly concerned to trace changing perceptions of the body as the site of sexual difference, but his argument is equally valid for any attempt to specify the "nature" of the body insofar as it is the origin of sex or sexuality. All of this is not to say that the body, sex, and sexuality do not exist. As Laqueur notes, we are in fact poised between our culturally determined perceptions of the body and our extra-linguistic sense of the "extraordinarily fragile, feeling, and transient mass of flesh with which we are all familiar" (12). Yet the body and the sexual are, finally, simply unknowable in the sense that our "knowledge" of them is constructed out of the cultural assumptions and the language in which such understanding is formulated, implicitly shaped by the uses to which such knowledge can be put. Sex, sexuality, and the body must finally be identified with what Lacan has called "the real"—that evanescent reality whose true nature, forever obscured by our formulations of it, can never be known.

In and of itself, this limitation does not pose insuperable problems for the representation of the sexual. As Fredric Jameson has argued, the same is true of "history," and the most frequently cited passage in *The Political Unconscious* can be used as a summary of the preceding points if we simply substitute *the sexual* for the term *history:* "History is *not* a text, not a narrative, master or otherwise, but . . . as an absent cause, it is inaccessible to us except in textual form, and . . . our approach to it and to the Real itself necessarily passes through its prior textualization, its narrativization in the political unconscious" (1981, 35). If, like history, the sexual is available to us only as a text, then, Jameson suggests, our task is to analyze the ways in which it is textualized, to examine the specific social beliefs and pressures, the "political unconscious," that creates and shapes this "text" that is all we can really know of sex and sexuality.

The sexual can thus be constituted in a variety of ways, and our concern must be to determine how the Victorians conceived of sex and sexuality. Stephen Heath asserts that the terms themselves emerge in a recognizable form during the nineteenth century, with *sexuality* taken as the individual's sexual desires and behaviors, and *sex* understood as an "area" of personal and cultural experience (1984, 8–9).[3] Even if Victorian terminology approximates our own, however, we should not assume that they read exactly the same content into it, that they perceived sex and sexuality in precisely the same ways as we do. As Heath argues, the Victorians attempted to limit sex to a concern with reproduction and to consider it as a largely medical topic. They were also aware, however, of a certain "pressure" of the sexual beyond such representations (13). This excess was itself represented in medicalized terms, so that sexuality not only was troped as the cause of various nervous disorders (male hypochondria, female hysteria) but was also seen, implicitly, as a nervous disorder itself. The sexual was thus conceived as "trouble, disorder, an ever-threatening disturbance of the regulation of the economy of the body—and of society with it" (20). Victorian responses to this characterization stressed regulation and delimitation. Beyond medicalization itself (the ideological and institutional containment of nonreproductive sexuality as an illness), the sexual was constrained and delimited through belief in the lack of sexual feeling in women (which could appear *only* as illness, as hysteria) and through normative models of masculine self-control (based on an economic ideal of the male sexual body as a balance between expenditure and conservation of seminal fluids) (18–23).

Heath explains both this characterization of the sexual as disorder and consequent attempts at ideological and social regulation as the result of an aporia, arguing that the term *sexuality* emerged before a full construction of the concept itself, so that "there is no idea of sexuality, no libido, no desire," (23) but only foreshadowings or traces of a "sexuality" that cannot yet be recognized. For Heath, the emergence of a fully developed idea of sexuality must wait for Freud. Even a brief glance at the Victorian novel, however, suggests that ideas of erotic experience and sexual desire are not entirely unformulated for the Victorians, even if they are not always overtly articulated, and it would seem more accurate to follow Foucault in situating the emergence of sex and sexuality as recognizable concepts in the early eighteenth century. As such, Victorian tropings of the sexual as disruptive and disorderly derive not from an inability to formulate the "nature" of sex and sexuality but precisely from a Victorian construction of sex and sexuality as chaotic. In order to understand the Victorian sense of the sexual as anarchic, whether this is conceived in relation to society or evidenced in the experience of the individual, we must first turn to the larger conceptual systems into which the idea of the sexual is inserted, the other concepts with which it interacts. As we shall see, if the sexual is troped as chaotic for the Victorians, this is in part because it is perceived as outside the orderly realm of "culture" or "civilization," associated instead with the disorder of "nature" and savage instincts. Victorian perceptions of sex and sexuality are thus intimately linked to their ideas of nineteenth-century Western industrial society itself, their notions of "culture" and "civilization."

SAVAGERY AND ITS DISCONTENTS

As Clifford Geertz has argued, "culture" is not a reified entity that creates institutions, social events, and behaviors but is, rather, "interworked systems of construable signs" (1973, 14), the context in which such institutions, events, and behaviors can be understood. Geertz's semiotic definition of culture insists on any given culture as a text, as a "historically transmitted pattern of meanings embodied in symbols, a system of inherited conceptions expressed in symbolic forms by means of which men communicate, perpetuate, and develop their knowledge about and attitudes toward life" (89). Every culture, then, provides its members with a conceptual map that allows them to interpret the world and enables them to act within it. One of the crucial features of the complex of meanings that forms a culture is that society's definition of "culture" itself, how it construes and delimits its conception of society.

Geertz's concept of culture reflects the cultural relativism of

Introduction

the twentieth century. The Victorians, in contrast, worked with a less fluid notion, defining "culture" in ways that, though still familiar to us, constructed the world and their place in it differently. For much of the century, *culture* was roughly synonymous with *civilization,* both terms implying a universal process of human development and the achieved state of social life that was the result of that process. Thus *culture,* whose original meaning was the tending of natural growth, and by extension, human development ("cultivation"), came to stand in the nineteenth century against an idea of undeveloped "nature," either in the sense of a physical world unaffected by human intervention or an essential "human nature" untouched by social refinement (Williams 1976, 77, 188). Similarly, the meaning of *civilization* developed in the nineteenth century beyond an idea of refined manners (the eighteenth-century sense of the term) to include the ideas of social order and ordered, which is to say "scientific," knowledge. "Civilization" was thus preeminently an idea of the implicit regulation of self and society, a notion of coherent behavioral, social, and epistemological rules and structures that stood in opposition to the "barbaric" or the "savage," the chaotic absence of such structures (Williams 1976, 48). Such distinctions between culture and nature, civilized and savage, organized the Victorian universe, and to understand Victorian ideas of sex and sexuality as inherently anarchic, we must see how those ideas intersect with Victorian conceptions of culture or civilization. Such intersections are clearest on the fringes of civilized society, evident at two places where civilization and barbarism, culture and nature meet: Africa and the psyche.

The distinction between civilized and savage is perhaps nowhere more apparent than in the imperial project, where the opposed terms are literalized in the geography of the world. As Patrick Brantlinger has demonstrated, even before the militarized period of high imperialism at the end of the century, British encounters with the non-Western world were ideologically justified by an implicit logic of colonialism. Whether their aim was to convert native peoples or to explore unfamiliar territory or to develop trade, British missionaries and explorers grounded their enterprise on the implicit assumption that the process was inevitable. As representatives of civilization, their mission was to develop unimproved regions and barbaric races. The "savages" they encountered would thus be educated and elevated, brought closer to the developmental stage of civilized Europe (or, in the more pessimistic vision of the latter part of the century, simply fade away, inadvertently exterminated by the pressure of a superior race) (Brantlinger 1988, 19–45). This ideology found the perfect object in Africa, which seemed to the Englishman of the nineteenth century to be almost prehistorically primitive, a dark continent in need of the light of civilization (174).

The opposition of the civilized and the savage, however, is not simply diachronic, a question of the confrontation of two stages in a "universal" process of social development. It is also, implicitly, a synchronic encounter, a clash between various reified concepts that the Victorians distributed between the ideas of the civilized and the savage, ideas literally embodied in the European explorer and the African natives he encountered. Thus British industriousness was contrasted with native indolence, enlightened Western thought with primitive superstition, civilized order with the chaos of savage life.[4] Such perceptions served not only to characterize Africa but also to consolidate Victorian self-images. As Brantlinger notes, the idea of Africa helped to deny the possibility that "civilized man" possessed any "savage impulses," Africa providing a fertile ground for projection, a locus onto which such unacceptable qualities could be displaced (194). What is significant for our purposes, for understanding how the sexual is situated in relation to Victorian self-definitions, is that such impulses are so often erotic.

This becomes abundantly clear in the travel narrative of a twenty-three-year-old Englishman. During most of 1862, W. Winwood Reade journeyed through West Africa. His account of the trip, published a year later as *Savage Africa,* rather haphazardly identifies a number of goals for his voyage that would seem to define Reade as an explorer. As the advance guard of Western civilization, Reade plans to stay for a month or so among the Bapuku to "study man in a debased state," to find whether the gorilla is met with so far north (1863, 86–87), and to discover the falls of the Ncomo River (136). The actual discovery of the latter leads to a characteristic narrative effusion: "I could look round and say, 'Here have men striven to come, and none have succeeded but myself. For the first time the breath of a white man mingles with this atmosphere; for the first time a leathern sole imprints its pressure on this soil; for the first time a being who has heard

Grisi, and who faintly remembers the day when he wore kid-gloves, invades this kingdom of the cannibal and the ape' " (154). The only hitch in this tiny, triumphant moment in the imperial enterprise is that, his shoes having been ruined earlier, Reade is forced to make his momentous landing in a pair of carpet slippers. In fact, the presence of these carpet slippers in the African interior signals an implicit insistence on the comforts of home, the need to import England to, and impose it on, Africa. But they also suggest a more unusual aspect to Reade's narrative, a different reason to go to Africa. As Reade notes in the preface to the volume, he cannot really be considered an explorer: "If I have any merit, it is that of having been the first young man about town to make a *bona fide* tour in Western Africa; to travel in that agreeable and salubrious country with no special object, and at his own expense; to *flâner* in the virgin forest; to flirt with pretty savages; and to smoke his cigar among cannibals." Since the African climate is, for Reade, far from "salubrious," continually associated with disease and death, one may suspect a certain facetiousness here, a calculated modesty about his achievements. The narrative as a whole, however, seems to confirm this characterization of Reade as a dilettante adventurer, as a "young man about the jungle," if only because he does in fact take every available opportunity to flirt with "pretty savages."

One such episode is his encounter with Ananga, daughter of Quenqueza, "King of the Rembo." Ananga is strikingly beautiful and "as chaste, as coquettish, and as full of innocent mischief, as a girl of sixteen would have been in England" (188). It is with Ananga that Reade discovers "a new and an innocent pleasure—one which you, in your wretched Europe, can never hope to enjoy" (192). It is an "epoch" in a man's life, he argues, to bestow a kiss on lips "which tremble with love for the first time." Imagine then, he continues, what it must be like to kiss someone who "has never dreamt that human lips could be applied to such a purpose" (192). The experiment is not, at least initially, a success. Having heard many stories of white cannibals and knowing that snakes moisten their victims with their lips before feeding on them, Ananga's first impression is that Reade intends to eat her, and she flees. She is persuaded to return, however, and to "offer her pouting lips" in "atonement of her folly." What ensues is not stated, the episode concluding instead with a coy assertion. Although "the negro intellect is not yet in a fit state to grasp the doctrinal mysteries of our Church," Reade says, a mission to diffuse *this* practice among the natives "would meet with eminent success, and would make innumerable female converts" (193). If Reade has brought his carpet slippers to Africa, this is perhaps because it seems to be one huge bedroom.

If Reade's narrative thus establishes Africa as the locus of the sexual, African sexuality initially appears almost prelapsarian. The simple pleasure of his encounter with Ananga, unavailable in "wretched Europe," seems to be predicated precisely on an ideal of the innocence of the noble—and nubile—savage, a traditional representation of the naive sexuality of the pastoral state of nature. In the context of the larger narrative, however, this perspective appears finally as a brief, although fairly typical, moment of ambivalence about civilization. Generally, Reade sees Africa not as a garden but as a wilderness, not as a site of naive pleasure but as a locus of "uncivilized" debauchery. Considering African sexual mores as a whole, Reade is later provoked to a vehement outburst against native sexuality. Are these, he asks with evident disgust, the noble savages that philosophers would have us imitate: "Must we instruct our children in vice at the tenderest possible age and sell them for marriage as soon as they arrive at puberty? . . . Must we place no restraints upon our passions; but abandon our youth to dissipation and debauchery, that we may have grey hairs on young heads, and all the foul diseases which spring from the diet and habits of a brute? For so does man in an uncivilized condition" (263).

Reade's link between uncontrolled sexuality and an "uncivilized condition" suggests that when the opposition of the cultural and the natural is displaced onto a colonial geography, a civilized Europe and a savage Africa, Africa becomes the continent of the body and of sexual passion in contrast to the erotic restraint of the civilized nations. Although Ananga's demure behavior would seem to be more prim than primitive, Reade resolves the anomaly by characterizing such behavior in English terms ("as chaste as a girl of sixteen would have been in England") and approaching Africa generally as a land of unrestrained sexuality, a massively enlarged version of the Haymarket. Reade's sexual cartography is elaborated in a later aside. In Africa, he asserts, one longs finally for the company of a "woman": "It is true that there are girls here who have such sweet smiles, such dark, voluptuous eyes, such fond, caressing ways, that one cannot help loving them; but only as one loves a child, a dog, or a singing-bird. They can gratify the desire of a libertine, but they cannot inspire a passion of the soul, nor feed that hunger of love which must sometimes gnaw the heart of a refined and cultivated man" (307). The Negress might be beautiful, he continues, able to create a sensation in the demi-monde, "but where is the coy glance, the tender sigh, the timid blush? where is the *intellect,* which is the light within the crystal lamp, the genius within the clay? No, no; the negress is not a woman; she is a parody of woman; she is a pretty toy, an affection-ate brute—that is all" (307).

It is precisely in the rather extraordinary racism of Reade's views that his conception of sexuality becomes clear. If Reade continually insists throughout his narrative on the inferior intel-lect of the African, this is because the African, here the African woman, is the body, the European the mind. Thus the pretty sav-age can offer only the pleasures of sex and sensuality in contrast to the spiritual love that is the province of the cultivated. It is thus precisely her coyness, her romantic suppression of the physical, that makes the European female a woman instead of a brute. In the largest sense, then, sex and the body are posited as other than civilization, easily conflated with the larger image of racial, cul-tural, and geographic alterity that is Africa.

This association of the sexual and the corporeal with uncivi-lized life means that the sexual, like savage existence itself, is seen as inherently chaotic, outside of the order of civilization. The equation of sexuality with savagery and the disorder associated with both are strikingly encapsulated in Reade's culminating image of Africa. Fancifully asserting that the continent resembles a woman facing America with a huge burden on her back, he sum-marizes Africa in an inverted blazon. Africa is "a Woman whose features, in expression, are sad and noble, but which have been degraded, distorted, and rendered repulsive by disease. Whose breath is perfumed by rich spices and by fragrant gums; yet through all steals the stench of the black mud of the mangroves, and the miasma of the swamps. Whose lap is filled with gold, but beneath lies a black snake, watchful and concealed. From whose breasts stream milk and honey, mingled with poison and with blood" (487). Clearly, this is not the "woman" one finds in Europe but rather a more unconscious image in which "woman" figures a multiple otherness: the feminine as sexual and reproductive body as the uncivilized. The very conflation of the images (and their implicit deconstruction of the cultural fiction of the European woman as spiritual and sexless) suggests a sexual anxiety so extreme that it verges on nausea, an anxiety that can be expressed only through the passage's baroque grotesqueness. Thus Reade's imagery itself enacts the central anxiety that is at the core of the passage: the fear of the chaotic. For the horror of this conflated image of sexuality, the corporeal, and Africa is less their continual association with decay, disease, and death than the images they provoke of disorder and chaotic mingling: the uncanny blending of perfume and miasmal stench; the mixed stream of milk and poison, honey and blood; even the erasure of gender difference in the image of Africa as phallic mother.[5] Confronting the chaos of the savage and of the sensual body, even the syntactic order of Reade's language collapses into sentence fragments, the paragraph's parallel clauses barely held together by anaphora ("whose . . ."). As Reade's vertiginous summary suggests, Victorian ideas of the civilized and the savage, of culture and nature, stand as highly charged synecdoches for a complex of conceptual opposites, a distribution of qualities that serves to define and delimit Victorian society. What is significant for our purposes is that civilized order is seen as the realm of the mind, the spiritual, and love in contrast to the chaotic disorder of the body, the physical, and sex.

This exclusion of sexuality and the body from the Victorian notion of civilization, a crucial aspect of Victorian self-fashioning, almost immediately shows signs of conceptual strain because the opposition of "culture" and "nature" is not as pure or as stable as Reade wants to insist. The body and sexuality exist in Europe too, if only in the libertine and the demimonde, as Reade is forced implicitly to admit and as his own behavior in Africa confirms, a fact that may account for the extremity of his sexual anxiety. Reade's encounter with Ananga is predicated precisely on the ideal of the "young man about town," a cultural stereotype that both undercuts Reade's attempt to limit the sexual to Africa and undermines his repudiation of sexuality. As a result, the incident disrupts and reverses the ideas of civilized *aphanisis* (the absence of sexual desire) and savage sexuality, with Reade acting the role of the urbane roué, the connoisseur of sexual experiences, and Ananga positioned as the reluctant (and hence implicitly passionless) virgin, a "natural" innocent. As such contradictions at the core of Reade's text suggest, in order to posit a conception of culture that excludes sex and the body, the Victorians must employ an additional, and more subtle, conceptual strategy, an insistence less on the absolute opposition of civilized man and savage sexuality than on civilization as precisely the restraint of the sexual. In a sense the conflict is played out internally, transposed onto the cultivated individual, who must then confront the savage impulses within.

This internal conflict is implied by Reade's own experiences in Africa, but it is far clearer in a late formulation, one that in fact occurs in the 1930s—Freud's *Civilization and Its Discontents.* "Civilization" *(Kultur)* is, Freud argues, the "achievements and the regulations that distinguish our lives from those of our animal ancestors" ([1930] 1961, 89). He then identifies two goals of civilization: the protection of humanity from (physical) nature and the regulation of social relations. Explaining the latter concept, Freud emphasizes that civilization is built upon the renunciation of instinct, especially the suppression of the "aggressive instincts," but culture is also antithetical to the sexual instincts. In fact, the founding moment of civilization occurs with the advent of sexual repression. The control of fire, Freud asserts in a famous footnote, came at a particular historical moment. When he encountered fire, primal man had the habit of satisfying an "infantile desire" by putting it out "with a stream of his own urine." At its core, the significance of this "habit" is sexual. There is "no doubt" that the tongues of flame were viewed phallically, and the act of putting out the fire was thus a "kind of sexual act with a male, an enjoyment of sexual potency in a homosexual competition. The first person to renounce this desire and spare the fire was able to carry it off with him and subdue it to his own use. By damping down the fire of his own sexual excitation, he had tamed the natural force of fire. This great cultural conquest was thus the reward for his renunciation of instinct" (90n).

This is certainly an improbable moment in human history, as Freud himself admits, but it is precisely the fantastic quality of the assertion that suggests the ideological underpinnings of Freud's analysis. The point is not simply that Freud confirms the Victorian antithesis between civilization and the sexual but how he constructs and construes this opposition, for Freud's discussion of the inauguration of civilization depends on a curious logic. If Freud stresses the birth of civilization as the advent of control over nature, the act of pissing on the fire to put it out would seem to demonstrate such control. Freud's argument, however, takes a more circuitous route. The "cultural conquest" of fire is preceded by and derives from an internal conquest, the "damping down" of the fire within. Man's control over nature thus depends on his control over himself. As such, "civilization" not only involves the renunciation of the sexual instincts, it *is* this renunciation. Based on this conception of internal regulation, Freud's argument not surprisingly goes on to parallel Reade's in its insistence on civilization as, in part, an idea of order (93) to which the sexual instincts are juxtaposed as disruptive and disorderly forces.

Freud's argument, however, does not really explain the origins of civilization or civilized repression, as a second glance at his logic reveals. Freud begins with an analogy, the metaphoric continuity of man and nature. Thus the anthropomorphic "tongues" of flame are also phalluses, the similarity of man and fire allowing their "homosexual competition," and sexual excitement, in an additional parallel, is itself a "fire." By positing the similarity of man and fire, Freud can stress the birth of civilization as the separation of man from nature, as the point where the link between the two becomes metaphoric—that is, only linguistic. And the moment at which the opposition of man and nature is created as man assumes control over the material world is also the moment at which man himself is divided between sexual desire and self-control, the creation of an internal difference between desire and renunciation. Significantly, the origins of this internal division are unexamined, and the psychologized splitting of the individual between the "natural force" of the instincts and a "civilized" capacity for renunciation would seem to depend less on any inevitable psychic development than on Freud's implicit insistence on, and belief in, this distinction itself. Assuming the difference it attempts to prove, Freud's argument is finally tautological.

As such, repression can be seen not as an inherent fact of the psychic mechanisms of the individual but as a socially constructed and induced phenomenon. This is not to say that people have never been, or are not now, repressed but to assert that Freud's reified notion of repression (and the experience of "repression" itself) are products of Victorian ideology, productions that parallel rather than ground the cultural logic of nineteenth-century imperialism. In other words, the civilizing project of colonialism cannot really be justified by the inherent superiority of the civilized (because repressed) man who imposes civilization on the "natives" in the form of a (reified) instinctual repression. Rather, colonialism and repression can be better understood as homologous creations of Victorian ideology's dependence on binary thinking. In both cases reality is constructed through the production of difference, the distinction and reification of concepts such as *mind* and *body, rational* and *instinctual,* which are then distributed across the world or within the individual as antagonistic states or forces. Both colonialism and Freudian psychology then proceed to define *civilization* as the imposition of rational order on the disordered and unregulated, whether the chaotic is portrayed as the non-Western world or the instincts. As it happens, the parallel is drawn by Freud himself. Personifying civilization, Freud compares its insistence on restriction of the sexual instincts to the colonial process: "Civilization behaves towards sexuality as a people . . . does which has subjected another one to its exploitation. Fear of a revolt by the suppressed elements drives it to stricter precautionary measures" (104).

Freud is discussing the "cost" of renunciation here, which produces the "discontents" of civilization, and the passage manifests a certain unhappiness with both repression and colonialism. Despite his ambivalence, however, Freud's argument implicitly rests on a belief in civilized repression, on the difference between civilized and savage people. Not surprisingly, however, Freud, like Reade, encounters some difficulties in maintaining the distinction. If the intent of the metaphors of internal and external fires is to stress the difference between man and nature, these metaphors can nonetheless be read the other way: as evidence of the continuity of man and nature. This continuity is illustrated even in the contemporary individual, who, Freud notes, is at heart a "savage beast" (112). Repression, Freud must admit, is a tenuous victory, and civilization is continually threatened with disintegration because instinctual passions are stronger than reason. This perception explains Freud's emphasis on history, his concern to pinpoint the origins of civilization, even though this historical perspective is not essential to his overall argument. In order to preserve the ideas of civilization and civilized persons and to maintain an opposition between them and the concepts of the savage or of "human nature," Freud, like Reade, projects the conflict elsewhere. If in Reade's case the clash is displaced spatially, projected outward onto a world geography, in Freud's case it is displaced temporally, backward in time. Thus, whatever the difficulties in insisting on civilized repression in any contemporary individual, the distinction of civilized renunciation and sexual instinct is nonetheless ensured by imagining an irrevocable historical moment when the difference came into being.

Such projections and displacements lead us to the heart of Victorian perceptions of the sexual. If Victorian self-definition rests on an idea of nineteenth-century English society as "civilization," this idea is constructed through the production and elaboration of binary oppositions. Thus Victorian "culture," the realm of the mind, the spiritual, the rational, is defined through its difference from "nature," the realm of the body, the physical, the instinctual. Seen as biological impulses and animal instincts, the sexual is located outside of culture in order to define culture. Victorian anxiety about sex and sexuality, however, derives not simply from the notion that they are other than civilization and the civilized person and that, as a result, sex and sexuality are inherently chaotic, associated with the "disorderly" realm of nature. As Reade's and Freud's texts suggest, the sexual also represents one of the places where conceptual problems emerge in the Victorian worldview. For sex and sexuality continually appear in the heart of civilization and in the civilized individual, deconstructing the opposition of culture and nature and producing strains in the conceptual framework on which Victorian society is based. Not surprisingly, then, the Victorians see sex and sexuality as chaotic not only in their essence but in their effects, as forces that continually threaten to shatter the distinction between civilized and savage or culture and nature. Whether associated with the practices of "savages" or articulated as repressed "instinct," the sexual is implicitly, if often unconsciously, seen by the Victorians as precisely resistant to the production of the differences that define the text of Victorian culture.

This perception is nowhere clearer than in nineteenth-century readings of the effects of sex and sexuality. An 1806 review of the love poetry of Thomas Moore published in the Methodist *Eclectic Review* anticipates the Victorian sense of the threat posed by the sexual: "The danger lies in dallying with sin, and with sensual sin above all other: it works, it winds, it wins its way with imperceptible, with irresistible insinuation, through all the passages of the mind, into the innermost recesses of the heart; while it is softening the bosom, it is hardening the conscience; while, by its exhilaration, it seems to be spiritualizing the body, it is brutalizing the soul, and by mingling with its eternal essence, it is giving *immortality* to impotent unappeasable desires, it is engendering 'the worm that dieth not,' it is kindling 'the fire that is not quenched' " (814).

The passage is striking because of what is implied in the triumph of sin: the erasure of difference. Any individual, it suggests, is a dual being, a collection of related binary oppositions: soul and body, the spiritual and the "brutal," the eternal and the temporal. Despite such innate corruption, a heart hardened to sin and an alert conscience will keep the spiritual and the physical distinct and ensure the dominance of the former. The problem with the enticing insinuations of sin, however, is the collapse of distinction between the two realms. Affected by sentimentality, the body becomes falsely "spiritualized"; tainted by the sensual, the soul is "brutalized." Worse still, sensual sin confuses the temporal and the eternal: the evanescent demands of the physical mingle with the immortal essence of the soul. Victorian anxiety about sensuality would seem to rest in part on this vision of sexual desire not merely as a spiritual danger but as a force that erases crucial distinctions.

Moreover, as Derrida has demonstrated, any binary opposition is implicitly hierarchical, involving the superior valuation of one of the terms. Thus, despite a certain ambivalence about civilization, both Reade and Freud implicitly assume the superiority of culture to nature, of the civilized person to the savage, and of repression to the instincts. Victorian conceptions of sexuality also stress the potential of the sexual to disrupt such hierarchical relations. The danger of sin, then, for the anonymous reviewer is not simply that it blurs crucial distinctions but that it also inverts the proper hierarchical relation of the spiritual and the physical. As soul and body become more alike, it is the body that gains ascendancy, and desire becomes immortal while the soul "dies to salvation." Sensual sin leads not only to spiritual death but to revolution and chaos, not just the collapse of internal differences but the overthrow of psychological hierarchies.

Such a perspective is not confined to religious formulations of the effects of sexuality. The dangerous potential of the sexual is confirmed, for example, in Thackeray's discussion of authorial self-restraint in *Vanity Fair*. Defending his presentation of Becky Sharp, the narrator argues that he has sketched her in a "genteel and inoffensive" manner. The narrative gaps in her history, he argues, are entirely justified:

> In describing this syren, singing and smiling, coaxing and cajoling, the author, with modest pride, asks his readers all round, has he once forgotten the laws of politeness, and showed the monster's hideous tail above water? No! Those who like may peep down under waves that are pretty transparent, and see it writhing and twirling, diabolically hideous and slimy, flapping amongst bones, or curling round corpses; but above the water line, I ask, has not everything been proper, agreeable, and decorous, and has any the most squeamish immoralist in Vanity Fair a right to cry fie? When, however, the syren disappears and dives below, down among the dead men, the water of course grows turbid over her, and it is labour lost to look into it ever so curiously. They look pretty enough when they sit upon a rock, twanging their harps and combing their hair, and sing, and beckon to you to come and hold the looking-glass; but when they sink into their native element, depend on it those mermaids are about no good, and we had best not examine the fiendish marine cannibals, revelling and feasting upon their wretched pickled victims. And so, when Becky is out of the way, be sure that she is not particularly well employed, and that the less said about her doings the better. ([1847-48] 1963, 617-18)

Thackeray does not say that the material he is deleting is sexual, but what is striking about the passage is the sexual anxiety that suffuses it. Having been identified elsewhere in the novel with Circe, the magically enchanting woman who turns men into beasts, Becky is transformed here into a mermaid, one of the traditional images of woman as a temptress whose allure leads men to destruction (Auerbach 1987, 90-94). Sexuality, the passage suggests, is aligned with the destructive forces unleashed in nature, with animal impulses and death.

A potent emblem of the dangerous power of sexuality itself, the mermaid is also an apt image of the individual overwhelmed by sensual desires. Unlike the rational human being, whose self-control insists on the difference between culture and nature through the denial of his or her instinctual side, the mermaid erases such distinctions. If the waterline separates the civilized world of the land from the natural world of the ocean, she transgresses this boundary, existing simultaneously in both, just as her behavior combines the accomplishments of the drawing room (harp playing and song) with the dietary preferences of that most benighted of savages, the cannibal. At once woman and sea-creature, alluring and repulsive, she evades categorization, representing the collapse of the distinction between human and animal, civilized and savage, that occurs when the individual is unable to restrain his or her biological urges. This erasure of difference derives, once again, from the disruption of a psychological and moral hierarchy. At first glance the mermaid seems to be a perfect symbol of the binary, hierarchical nature of the civilized person—she is human above and "marine creature" below both the waist and the "surface." This dominance of the civilized, however, is only apparent. She is governed, finally, not by reason or self-control but by savage impulses; the water is her "native element," and she is "about no good" there. Like the individual overcome by sensuality, she represents the inversion of the ascendancy of reason over instinct.

Victorian perceptions of the disruptive potential of sexuality do not stop with a sense of its tendency to dismantle such binary oppositions as culture and nature or civilized and savage. As its ability to invert or confound hierarchical relations implies, it also threatens another aspect of Victorian ideology—the belief in taxonomic structures, most notably the class system. It is not accidental that, for the Englishman of the nineteenth-century, the French revolution was associated not simply with political upheaval but with moral laxity, for Victorian ideas of the sexual implicitly assume that the effects of sexuality on society are isomorphic to its impact on the individual (Weeks 1981, 27; Trudgill 1976, 30–31). Not just psychologically but socially, unrestrained sexuality is associated with the rise of dark forces from the depths, with a nightmarish democracy in which everyone and everything become the same, with the collapse of hegemony and the dissolution of taxonomy. To understand this additional troping of the sexual as chaotic, we must consider Victorian conceptions of taxonomy, the ways in which classification is used to order the Victorian universe. In other words, we must now consider Darwin.

TAXONOMIES

The Victorian tendency to organize the world into categories is evident in a number of contemporary scientific or pseudoscientific disciplines from linguistics to phrenology, but it is clearest in the science that came, in the course of the century, to call classification into question: biology. Using the now-familiar categories established during the eighteenth century, Victorian morphology organized all living beings into a complicated system of groups and subgroups: classes, orders, families, genera, species, and varieties. Curiously, the taxonomic habits of mind evident in such a system are nowhere more apparent than in Darwin, the man who did the most to undermine the rationale for biological classification. Although Darwin's *Origin of Species* challenges the ideas of the independent creation and immutability of species upon which biological taxonomies are based, his discussion also demonstrates the powerful hold of taxonomy on Victorian thought.

In this context the revolutionary aspect of Darwin's thought is the notion of descent with modification, the idea that species are created through a series of progressive variations, naturally selected, from a common parent. The result is a conceptual revolution in biological thinking, for the effect of Darwin's assertions is to insert temporality into a previously fixed and static system, presenting a vision of the natural world as continually changing. Moreover, beyond the difficulties posed for the traditional biological taxonomy by this mutability, Darwin's theory challenges the possibility of classification itself. If, as Darwin asserts at the end of the work, all living beings may have descended from a single primordial form through a series of slight variations upon variations over countless ages, then distinctions between species, genera, and so forth cannot be firmly maintained. As Darwin realizes, if we could simultaneously see all present and extinct life-forms, the vision would make taxonomic classification impossible. Given the slightness of the variations between various groups, all organic beings would blend indistinguishably into an "inextricable chaos" ([1859] 1985, 438).

Introduction

The implications of Darwin's theory were not lost on his contemporaries. Writing in 1889, Edward Carpenter affirms that the doctrine of evolution obliterates distinctions: "There is a continuous variation from the mollusc to the man—all the lines of distinction run and waver—classes and species cease to exist—and Science, instead of many, sees one thing. What then is that one thing? Is it a mollusc, or is it a man, or what is it?" (94). Evolution, Carpenter notes, involves the destruction of Science, whose distinctions are simultaneously revealed as arbitrary and obliterated. Modern commentators have confirmed Carpenter's reading of Darwin. Thus James Krasner argues that Darwin's use of a fluid, shifting model of visual perception as the basis for description in *The Origin* is designed to demonstrate nature as a state of evolutionary flux and to subvert the traditional categorization of species (Krasner 1990; see also Cannon 1968, 160). Despite this revolutionary vision, Darwin's own thought reveals a desire for traditional taxonomy even as it recognizes the inadequacy of such classifications, *The Origin of Species* being grounded, as Gillian Beer repeatedly stresses, in contemporary modes of ordering experience (1983, 9, 37, 47). It is precisely Darwin's attempts to salvage biological classification in the face of the radical implications of his own theory that suggests the importance of taxonomy for the Victorians.

Darwin uses several strategies to recuperate the possibility of taxonomy. The first is to insist on the distinctness of species at any one period. If, Darwin asks, species have descended from other species by "insensibly fine" gradations, "why is not all nature in confusion instead of the species being, as we see them, well defined?" (205). In other words, Darwin must explain why species do not present the sort of undifferentiated continuum apparent in climate or geography, where height or depth or climatic conditions "graduate away insensibly" (208). Darwin provides a number of answers to the problem such as the slowness of the process of natural selection and the tendency of new variations to eliminate previous intermediate types. To insist on the distinctness of species at any given moment, however, really only transfers Darwin's problem to the historical dimension, for a historical overview would reveal precisely a picture of insensibly fine gradations between species, presenting nature as a "chaos" that evades classification.

In effect, Darwin solves the problem of classificatory difference by creating a distinction between significant and insignificant amounts of difference. All of Darwin's argument rests on the implicit notion that, below a certain threshold, difference does not matter. In other words, while, seen historically, beings would present an unbroken continuum that cannot be segmented, Darwin implicitly assumes the importance of taxonomic classification and thus focuses on the point at which a sufficient number of differences have emerged to allow classification. This assumption is apparent in Darwin's recurrent metaphors themselves, particularly in the use of the word *gradation,* which implies distinct grades (even if, as with climate, these are "insensibly fine," below the threshold of human perception). By the same token, Darwin's use of the older metaphors of the scale of nature and of nature as a chain (of which the various species form the links) subtly insists on the distinctness of species, even if such metaphors have been stripped of their earlier association with a divinely mandated hierarchy. A similar stress on distinctness is evident in Darwin's use of "steps" or "stages" to characterize intermediate forms between species. Despite the implications of his theory, Darwin thus subtly insists on older habits of thought, on nature not as an unbroken continuum but as discrete, albeit interrelated, categories (grades, steps, stages, links).

Darwin's insistence on the value of taxonomy, on the importance of classification, is clearest, however, at the point where he comes closest to presenting the antitaxonomic implications of evolutionary theory. Positing a simultaneous vision of every biological form that has ever lived, Darwin notes that it would be "impossible to give definitions by which each group could be distinguished from other groups" (413), since they would blend together. Nonetheless, he insists, a "natural classification" would still be possible. Reverting to his recurrent metaphor of a tree as a model for descent, Darwin insists that most of the forms distinguishing each group could be picked out, just as "in a tree we can specify this or that branch, though at the actual fork the two unite and blend together" (414). Since one could just as easily read the tree as a model of unbroken continuity, Darwin's stress on the distinctness of the branches suppresses the anticlassificatory implications of his theory, implicitly insisting on a taxonomic model of nature.

Thus Darwin can, at the end of the work, argue that evolutionary theory will actually aid in biological classification, uncovering the "law" of descent with modification that underlies the system and allowing "systematists" to place their classifications on a "natural" basis by helping them to focus on the characteristics that best mark the differences and affinities of groups of beings. Similarly, Darwin's work allows for the definition of such categories as families, genera, and species, since the larger groups are distinguished from each other by a greater degree of difference than exists between the smaller groups, a fact that also allows a clearer definition of *species,* since the term can now be defined as a certain degree of difference from related forms.

Darwin's final grounding of morphology in difference, in the difference between degrees of difference, suggests his stress on the importance of ordering and classifying the world, a stress that reflects contemporary perceptual strategies. As such, even before the rise of Social Darwinism, it is not surprising to find contemporary notions of human society predicated on the same set of taxonomic assumptions. As Cynthia Russett has noted, under the pressure of increasing social change, the eighteenth-century balance between a perception of the differences between humans and a stress on the commonality of human beings gave way in the nineteenth century to an emphasis on differentiation in which "categories hardened and were made permanent" (1989, 6). Unlike Darwinian biology, which divorces classification from the earlier assumption that the scale of nature is also a vertical ranking of superior and inferior beings, the nineteenth-century emphasis on the taxonomic ordering of groups in society is also a stress on hierarchy.

This insistence on sociological classification is nowhere clearer than in Henry Mayhew's monumental study of the working classes, *London Labour and the London Poor* (1861–62), for what is most striking in Mayhew is the continual proliferation of categories. The work presents a panoramic vision of the working class as sets of groups and subgroups in which everyone from chimney sweeps to costermongers, dog stealers to forgers, is labeled, categorized, and assigned a place. Thus, in Bracebridge Hemyng's section on "Prostitution in London," the analysis of London prostitutes is relentlessly taxonomic, continually organizing and subdividing its subjects into various "classes" and "races." The women he studies are first classed as professionals or amateurs, and the professionals are then subdivided into "seclusives" (who live in private houses), board lodgers, and those who live in lodging houses, the last group further distinguished into subgroups according to various incidental factors ("bunters," who abscond without paying rent, vs. "swindlers," who rob their clients).

It is in the very arbitrariness of these latter categories that the Victorian impulse to classify becomes most apparent. Nor is it entirely accidental that this impulse seems to take on a particular urgency here, in the section dealing with prostitution. For sexuality, from a Victorian perspective, implicitly uncovers an ideological conflict at the heart of ideas of social class. Beginning in the eighteenth century, Western culture was marked by a shift from belief in a caste system, in which differences between individuals in society are seen as innate, a matter of inborn difference, to the idea of social class, which views differences in rank as the result of a process of differentiation from a common sameness (Birken 1988, 4–5; Williams 1976, 52). This "democratization" of the idea of the social order was not absolute, however. Rather, it coexisted uneasily with earlier ideas, so that Victorian notions of class are profoundly conflicted. On the one hand, perceptions of class incorporated ideas of caste, so that social class was seen not only as a difference in degree but also as a difference in kind. Founded on the earlier assumption of the quasi-ontological difference between social strata, the class system reflected a sense that members of other social classes were fundamentally different by nature from members of one's own class, almost "another species" (Marcus [1966] 1985, 146). On the other hand, newer ideas of common humanity, of rank as a potentially mutable difference in degree, also underlie the Victorian class system. Sex and sexuality, which can be enacted across class boundaries, bring the latter notions to the fore, posing a threat to Victorian belief in the validity of social classifications.

The clash between sexuality and the social taxonomy emerges, for example, in Hemyng's interview with one prostitute. Ostensibly presented to exemplify the abandonment of womanly modesty that results from such an occupation, the interview inadvertently uncovers an entirely different set of concerns. Noting that she is very often sad, the anonymous speaker goes on to note: "Well! we don't fret that we might have been ladies, because we never had a chance of that, but we have forfeited a position nevertheless, and when we think that we have fallen, never to regain that which we have descended from, and in some cases sacrificed everything for a man who has ceased to love and deserted us, we get mad" (Mayhew [1862] 1968, 219). A few lines later, however, this woman articulates a radically different version of the harlot's progress: "Strange things happen to us sometimes: we may now and then die of consumption; but the other day a lady friend of mine met a gentleman at Sam's [a popular cafe], and yesterday morning they were married at St. George's, Hanover Square. The gentleman has lots of money, I believe, and he started off with her at once for the Continent. It is very true this is an unusual case; but we often do marry, and well too; why shouldn't we, we are pretty, we dress well, we can talk and insinuate ourselves into the hearts of men by appealing to their passions and their senses" (219).

The contradictions of this interview are played out in Hemyng's discussion as a whole, which, generally concerned to show the inevitable personal and social decline of the "fallen" woman, is forced to admit that such women often advance socially, that "as often as not" they do indeed "marry well" (251). This conflict between the cultural stereotype of the prostitute as social outcast and the reality of possible upward social mobility points directly to the anxiety latent here. The problem is not so much social mobility itself as the deeper implication that class distinctions are not actually based on ontological differences. The "passions" of these gentlemen thus become "revolutionary" because they imply the fundamental biological equality of all women, the inherent similarity of all people. Seen through the eyes of desire, a *fille de joie* is the equal of a duchess. This suggests that the distinctions imposed by society are artificial, that women who "by birth" had no chance of being ladies, who have even "fallen" from their social position, can marry gentlemen, can become ladies. Such stories counter the ideology of class difference with an alternate notion that such distinctions are superficial, less important than the humanity and sexuality, the passions and senses, everyone shares. On the most profound level, then, Hemyng's subsequent discussion of the marriage of "Agnes W——," a middle-class prostitute, to a member of "an old Norfolk family" threatens one of the logical foundations of Victorian society, the illusion of the natural, inevitable status of such cultural taxonomies as social class. If sexual desire is so often associated for the Victorians with chaotic mingling and taxonomic inversion, this is in part because, at its core, sexuality represents a universal biological sameness without distinction or rank that implicitly questions the social categorizations on which Victorian culture is constructed.

It is not surprising, then, that such democratic implications are largely repressed by Victorian society. In the case of the prostitute, such perceptions are blocked by the cultural fiction that social mobility will only be downward, an inevitable descent of the social scale that literalizes one's internal "moral" decline. Having intimated that this is not always the case, Hemyng nonetheless concludes his discussion with a summary, the tale of a girl from the West End who sinks "from one stage to another" until she is "compelled to solicit in the streets to obtain a livelihood" (259–60). This narrative thus serves as an example of what Roland Barthes has called inoculation (1972, 150), the partial admission of an unpleasant truth in order to distract attention from its larger implications. Acknowledging the possibility of downward social movement and thus tacitly admitting that social class is not immutable, the stereotypical narrative of the "fallen" woman subtly prevents consideration of the classlessness of the sexual body, if only because the story is charted against, and assumes the validity of, the class structure.[6] Overtly presented as a cautionary tale designed to discourage illicit sexual activity, Hemyng's final narrative ultimately serves to mask the deeper ideological threat that sexual activity poses to Victorian assumptions about the social order.

Thus Hemyng struggles with the same problems that beset Darwin. In both cases there is a recognition that the taxonomy in question (whether social or morphological) does not actually inhere in the objects it classifies, and both writers retreat from the resulting vision of an undifferentiated continuum of individual beings, insisting on the possibility of classification. If, for Hemyng, sex and sexuality raise the specter of chaos, suggesting an underlying biological sameness that disrupts the ideology of the class system, Darwin's difficulties also stem, if only indirectly, from sex, from an attempt to reconcile an implicitly sexualized biology with a traditional taxonomy. By replacing the concept of the independent creation of species with the idea of descent with modification, Darwin moves generation and reproduction to the fore as the principles animating the natural world. The resulting argument that all life descends from a common progenitor grounds biology in an originary oneness, an assertion that continually threatens to collapse differentiation into a recognition of the sameness of a common ancestry. Thus, for both Hemyng and Darwin, social or scientific classification is undermined by a (repressed) idea of the biological world as "in-different," as resistant to differentiation.

The sexual is thus perceived as chaotic by the Victorians not only because, as we have seen, it is associated with the disorderly realm of nature but also because it is linked to an idea of the biological that problematizes classification. The latter perception extends the scandal of the sexual for the Victorians, complicating its troping as chaotic. If, for Reade and Freud, the sexual is seen as a natural force that disrupts the order of civilization, creating a social and behavioral chaos, for Darwin and Hemyng the "in-difference" of the biological realm creates a logical problem, a conceptual chaos. For Hemyng, however, the logical problem entails a social one, just as, in Reade and Freud, the eruption of sexuality in the civilized individual creates a conceptual dilemma, and these two associations of the sexual (with the anarchic and the in-different) are not, finally, distinct ideas but interconnected perceptions, like the conceptions of nature and biology from which they derive. At bottom, "nature" is seen as "disorderly" precisely because it does not demonstrate the distinctions and differences that constitute the "order" of "culture." By the same token, the idea of an undifferentiated biological realm implies disorder for the Victorians, the notion of a morphological or social continuum being perceived precisely as, in Darwin's phrase, "an inextricable chaos."

This association of the sexual not only with the disorderly but also with the in-different can extend our understanding of the problems posed by sex and sexuality to Victorian culture and literature. Finally, the Victorians see the sexual as dangerous not only because it threatens particular binary oppositions and taxonomies such as the distinction of culture and nature or the class system but because it challenges the possibility of binary oppositions and taxonomy themselves. To understand the threat that the sexual poses not only to particular ideological productions of Victorian culture but also to the conceptual structures out of which such formations are generated, we must now examine these structures, looking at what Jameson has called "the content of the form," the "meaning" of binarism and taxonomy themselves.

THE SEXUAL DISCRETION OF VICTORIAN FICTION

The significance of such structures is suggested by Judith Butler's critique of the nature/culture distinction: "The binary relation between culture and nature promotes a relationship of hierarchy in which culture freely 'imposes' meaning on nature, and, hence, renders it into an 'Other' to be appropriated to its own limitless uses, safeguarding the ideality of the signifier and the structure of signification on the model of domination" (1990, 37). Butler's point is not simply that this particular opposition is a hierarchical construction but also that binarism itself encodes certain assumptions. To begin with, just as culture is presumed to dominate nature, the construction of binary oppositions as the relation between a superior term and an inferior one is predicated on and legitimates a structure of domination. Binarism thus implicitly asserts the inevitability of power and subjugation. Moreover, just as "culture" imposes a meaning on "nature," any binary opposition implicitly insists on and conceals the process of signification that constitutes it, the imposition of "meaning" on uninterpreted materiality. As such, binarism represents the domination of signification over the "real," an insistence on the necessity and validity of meaning itself. In short, according to Butler, binarism grounds both domination and signification, power and meaning. We can go even further, however, and note that any binary opposition also assumes and insists on difference, the segmentation of the continuum of "reality." In a sense, to revert to Darwin's metaphor, binary oppositions stress the separate branches of the tree, suppressing attention to the fork where "the two unite and blend together." As such, binarism asserts the validity of difference itself. Finally, if binarism can be said to have a meaning, then taxonomy can be seen as a further articulation of that meaning, for classificatory systems simply elaborate and extend the ideas of differentiation, labeling, and hierarchical dominance inherent in binary oppositions.

If binary opposition and taxonomic classification are crucial conceptual structures for the Victorians, this is not simply because particular ideas, such as the class system or the contrast of culture and nature, are necessary to organize the text of Victorian culture. Binarism and taxonomy themselves provide the grammar out of which the text is written, and the meanings of this text are already encoded in its grammar: the belief in power, meaning, and difference. Questions of power, the political uses of this grammar in Victorian culture, have been extensively analyzed, and numerous critics have suggested the ways in which the principles of binarism and taxonomy were used by white middle-class Victorian men to construct and define the inferiority and alterity of women, people of color, and the working class.[7] I will touch on such issues, on the ways in which Victorian representations of sex and sexuality work to further the process of gender, race, and class domination, but my focus here is finally less on power than on the threat posed by the sexual to Victorian belief in difference and meaning, the other principles on which Victorian culture and literature are grounded.

If Victorian culture is based on a belief in difference, on the necessity and the validity of segmenting and organizing "the real," then the sexual, associated not only with the chaos of nature but also with a biological realm that resists differentiation, is finally problematic for the Victorians precisely because it subverts the very logic of difference on which the binary oppositions and taxonomies that structure the Victorian worldview are predicated. Thus, as we shall see in the chapters that follow, the difficulty of the sexual for Victorian novelists goes beyond the fact that it problematizes the distinction of culture and nature or suggests a human sameness that challenges the class structure. Finally, the Victorians implicitly associate sex and sexuality with the impossibility of any taxonomy and with the disruption of any opposition, from contemporary ideas of gender difference to the distinction of self and other. At its core, the chaotic in-difference of the sexual is seen as a challenge to the principle of differentiation by which the Victorians construct and organize the world.

As such, some of the reasons for the sexual reticence of Victorian fiction become clear. To begin with, if the sexual is suppressed in Victorian fiction, then such dangerous implications can be held in check, recognized only dimly if at all. The matter is more complicated than this, however. If we look back at Thackeray's refusal to narrate the sexual in *Vanity Fair,* we can now see that such reticence also insists on the idea of difference implicitly challenged by the sexual. The image of the mermaid not only suggests the fragility of the distinction between culture and nature in the face of sexuality but also threatens to erase difference itself. The overall intent of Thackeray's discussion, however, is to assert both the viability of the specific distinction and the very possibility of distinction. If the mermaid suggests that control of sexual impulses is precarious in the life of the individual, the erotic reserve of Thackeray's novel subtly demonstrates that such control is in fact possible, that the proper can be distinguished from the improper, that decorum can take precedence over instinct. The waterline discussed by Thackeray is also the division of text and subtext, an above and below of the narrative. "Proper, agreeable, and decorous," the text is the realm of law, the "laws of politeness" in this case, and the sphere of civilization and rational restraint. Sexual material must be relegated to the subtext, the "writhing, twirling" domain of chaos and "turbid water." There may be moments, the narrator admits, when the narrative becomes transparent, hinting at this subtext, but textual decorum insists on a distinction between the things that can be said openly and those that cannot and on a hierarchical, qualitative relation between the two. Sexual reticence thus seeks to control the destabilizing effects of sexual desire on the individual and society by providing a model of rational restraint, but it has the additional function of denying the logical implications of the sexual. By maintaining a hierarchical distinction between the proper and the improper, sexual reticence also demonstrates the possibility of binarism and taxonomy. At its core, the sexual discretion of Victorian fiction can be seen as an insistence on the validity of making distinctions.

There is a final reason for the sexual discretion of nineteenth-century English fiction, a reason associated less with Victorian perceptions of the antipathy of the sexual to the idea of difference than with an additional problem: the actual resistance of the sexual to the production of meaning. Finally, the problems of representing the sexual in the Victorian novel are an implicit recognition that the sexual *cannot* be represented, that it resists the imposition of significance, of meaning, on uninterpreted materiality, a process that not only underlies the creation of the text of Victorian culture, the Victorian view of the world, but also grounds novelistic representation itself. As such, if I began this discussion by comparing "the sexual" to Jameson's notion of "history," I must now articulate the differences between the two. Although the historical and the sexual are both available only as texts, the raw material of history—whatever we conceive it to be—is not directly antithetical to the construction of coherence, to the creation of that "text." Whether the "real" of history is taken to be events or actions or persons that exist prior to the imposition of such cultural constructions as causality or a linear concept of time, this raw material, while it may provide the basis for a number of competing narratives, does not itself seem to resist the process of textualization. In contrast, insofar as we can dimly and obliquely perceive it, the "real" of sex and sexuality, the raw material out of which we construct "the sexual," would seem to be diametrically opposed to representation, not only resisting but shattering any attempt to narrate it.

This point has been made by Leo Bersani, who argues, in a persuasive rereading of Freud, that the "essence" of sexuality is that it is "intolerable to the structured self." The simultaneously pleasant and unpleasant tension of sexual excitement occurs when the body is confronted by sensations and affective processes that exceed the normal range and disturb the organization of the self. By definition, then, sexuality is experienced as a "shattering" of the self; it is the result of the gap between external stimuli and "the development of ego structures capable of resisting, or in Freudian terms, of binding those stimuli" (Bersani 1986, 38). Thus the infant's susceptibility to the sexual, his or her polymorphous perversity, reflects the vulnerability of the child's ego defenses. Understood in this way, sexuality consists of incoherent and ineffable "vibrations of being." As a shattering of consciousness, a dissolution of the self, sexuality cannot be understood or articulated by the rational processes or linguistic structures of the consciousness it fractures.

Bersani goes on to argue that the implications of Freud's theory of infantile sexuality thus flatly contradict Freud's attempt to write sexuality as a progression through a series of stages culminating in the Oedipus complex, an endeavor that emerges as a "narrativization," an attempt to render sexuality intelligible, which parallels the ego's efforts to structure and domesticate the exciting stimuli that threaten it. Like all logical discourse, however, this narrativization involves a "desexualization" of consciousness, a rational binding of the chaotic agitations produced in the individual by sexuality. The "real" of sexuality evades such rational arguments. Unstateable and alogical, it can "at the most, be 'related to,' or 'inferred from,' or 'correspond to' a certain type of insistence in consciousness which *it is the function of linguistic articulation to miss*" (66, emphasis in original). In fact, the "nature" of sexuality is most apparent in the failure of attempts to articulate it; Freud's formulations of it continually collapse into contradictions and tautologies that reveal sexuality's resistance to logical statement. Sexuality, it would seem, shatters not only the individual but language and logic.

Thus the "real" of the sexual is not simply always other than its representation, like the "real" of the historical. Unlike the historical, the "real" of sex and sexuality also disrupts or resists any attempt to represent it.[8] Whether or not this ineffability is openly recognized or clearly perceived by any given culture, it must itself be reflected, however indirectly, in that culture's perceptions and constructions of the sexual. The contemporary response of writers like Norman O. Brown or Deleuze and Guattari, for example, is to acknowledge openly the chaotic flux of the sexual and then to posit it as a locus of personal or social liberation from the binding conceptual and political structures, the ideological productions, of modern culture. For the Victorians, however, the tendency of the sexual to dismantle or deconstruct any attempts to articulate it produces an entirely different reaction. Although it would be anachronistic to argue that the Victorians fully understood the ineffability of the sexual, the "unspeakability" of sex is nonetheless reflected in Victorian culture precisely through the troping of sex and sexuality as chaotic and disruptive forces, the Victorian constructions of the sexual that we have been examining. The texts of Reade and Freud, Darwin and Mayhew can finally be seen as textualizations, as not entirely successful attempts to insist on conceptual structures (the oppositions of culture and nature and of repression and instinct, the morphological and social taxonomies) intended to contain and delimit, even as they construct, the chaos of the sexual.

We can now understand another reason for the sexual discretion of Victorian fiction. Beyond the uses of erotic reticence to suppress or conceal the tendency of the sexual to disrupt both particular cultural beliefs and the general principles of binarism and taxonomy that shape Victorian ideology, beyond the function of such reticence in establishing the validity of the idea of difference itself, the sexual discretion of Victorian literature can also be seen as a problem of meaning, a certain difficulty of representation or an anxiety about, and resistance to, depiction of the sexual that reflects the very impossibility of such representation. As we shall see in chapter 5, this resistance is finally the fear that the sexual will destroy the novel itself.

To argue, however, that the Victorian novel simply employs a sexual reticence that is designed to minimize the effects of sex and sexuality or that reflects the difficulties of representing the sexual is to oversimplify the case. As D. A. Miller has demonstrated, although the novel itself is often seen as a realm of freedom beyond the control of social regulation, the representational conventions of nineteenth-century novels actually illustrate a "micro-politics" of social control. If the content of Victorian novels often critiques the powers of regulatory agencies and of social discipline, the practices of narrative omniscience and attention to detail produce precisely the sort of information, exact the sort of knowledge, on which such control is predicated (Miller 1988, 16–25). Thus, even if sexuality is excluded from the surface of most nineteenth-century novels, such works do not really demonstrate a simple repression of the sexual. Intimately concerned with love and marriage, the Victorian novel cannot completely ignore sexuality or desire, and these novels can be read as attempts to speak, and hence to define and constrain, sex and sexuality.[9] In a sense, the Victorian novel could be said not so much to repress sex and sexuality as to enact a process of "sexual surveillance," an attempt to produce and construct, and thereby control, the sexual. Thus Victorian novels must finally be read as projects for the management of sex and sexuality that attempt to define the irrational ineffability of the sexual and to suggest modes of restraining and regulating its destructive effects: its potential for disruption of the self, the social order, or the conceptual foundations of Victorian culture.

Our examination of these projects can begin with Jane Austen's *Pride and Prejudice*. Written at the start of the century, Austen's novel establishes the basic principles of the literary production of the sexual in the Victorian novels that follow it. Although constructions of the sexual in the Victorian novel are not uniform, with definitions of sex and sexuality and strategies for their management shifting during the course of the century and varying from novelist to novelist, *Pride and Prejudice* can nonetheless be seen as a pre-text for the works that come after it. Perceiving the sexual as anarchic, Austen deploys both a doctrine and a practice of erotic discretion that define the parameters of the presentation of sex and sexuality in Victorian fiction. If we are to understand sexual representation in the Victorian novel or the Victorian sense of the "imperfect pleasures" of sex and sexuality, it is to Jane Austen then that we must first turn.

CHAPTER 2

No Love for Lydia: The Construction of Repression in *Pride and Prejudice*

Charlotte Brontë was the first reader, but certainly not the last, to argue that Jane Austen's novels minimize not only sexual feeling but emotion in general: "The Passions are perfectly unknown to her; she rejects even a speaking acquaintance with that stormy Sisterhood; even to the Feelings she vouchsafes no more than an occasional graceful but distant recognition; too frequent converse with them would ruffle the smooth elegance of her progress" ([1850] 1968, 128). Overstated, Brontë's assertion has nonetheless become a commonplace of Austen criticism: both characters and author control their emotions, expressing only those feelings that are compatible with decorum, the rules of polite society. As such, *Pride and Prejudice* can serve as a pre-text for an examination of cultural representations of the sexual in the Victorian novel, for Austen's work has long been taken to represent the conflict of "feeling" and "politeness," the institution of the ideas of "civilization" or "culture" as psychological and behavioral codes that place strong emotion in general, and the sexual in particular, in the realm of "nature," outside the bounds of both polite society and the novel (Mudrick 1952, 262; Nardin 1973, 12–23; Babb 1962, 15–19).

Brontë is mistaken, however, when she insists that the passions are completely unknown to Austen. As Susan Morgan has argued, Austen's rejection of the sexual plots of eighteenth-century novels, their recurrent focus on the rape or seduction of the virgin,

37

stems not from prudery but from a liberating refusal to define the heroine only in sexual terms (1989, 23–55). In addition, sexual narratives still have their place in Austen, often shaping the destinies of the secondary characters. If only because the last third of *Pride and Prejudice* centers on such a story, the scandal of Lydia's elopement and cohabitation with Wickham, there is more sexuality, and certainly more emotion, in Austen than Brontë suggests. Rather than completely ignoring sex, *Pride and Prejudice* "manages" it, adumbrating both a conception of the sexual and a set of techniques for controlling and representing it that are more fully articulated in the Victorian novels that follow it. Implicitly associating sexuality and desire with disorder and the erasure of cultural distinctions, Austen provides an implicit rationale for the suppression of desire by the characters, a rationale that redefines sexual desire in a socially acceptable form. Moreover, Austen responds to the actual ineffability of the sexual, its resistance to representation, with a variety of narrative techniques that attempt to textualize, to define as well as to control, the "unspeakable." As such, Austen's novel will provide an early example of the "sexual repression" that characterizes Victorian fiction, although sexual repression must be understood here not as a preexisting psychic mechanism but as an ideological production: as the development, rather than the discovery, of an interiority for both the characters and the narratives of the Victorian novel.

TROPING THE SEXUAL: DISORDER AND IN-DIFFERENCE

We can begin, however, with Lydia, the least-repressed character in *Pride and Prejudice*. Although the details of Lydia's elopement are not directly narrated in the novel, the effects of her actions allow Austen to intimate what has taken place in London and to figure the chaos that Austen associates with sexuality. As has often been noted, Lydia's behavior is an obvious disruption of the social order whose consequences are most evident in Elizabeth and Jane's meditations on the "shame and humiliation" brought on the family and on their own diminished chances for marriage. The effects of Lydia's "fall," however, are even more pervasive and subtle than this, as Mrs. Bennet's reaction to the elopement reveals. When she receives the news, even the morally impervious Mrs. Bennet is "taken ill immediately," going into a fit whose effects are still evident several days later when Elizabeth returns with the Gardiners. As Mrs. Bennet notes to Mr. Gardiner, "I am frightened out of my wits; and have such tremblings, such flutterings, all over me, such spasms in my side, and pains in my head, and such beatings at heart, that I can get no rest by night nor by day" (Austen [1813] 1932, 288). Mrs. Bennet is neurasthenic, and such a somatic response is typical of her, but she is not the only character to be physically affected by the crisis. As Elizabeth notes, Jane does not look well, and Elizabeth herself has a strong physical reaction to the letter bearing the news. Watching her read the letter, Darcy is startled by Elizabeth's "pale face and impetuous manner," and she agrees to let Darcy send a servant after the Gardiners only because her knees "tremble under her" and she is so breathless that she is too "miserably ill" to go herself. Assuring Darcy that she is "quite well," merely distressed by some "dreadful news," she nonetheless bursts into tears (276–77).

Even if one does not dwell on the sexual content latent in such hysteric reactions, it is clear that Lydia's actions induce a complex somatic response in her mother and sisters. This is significant for two reasons. First of all, this emphasis on the body indirectly articulates what cannot otherwise be spoken: Lydia's sexual actions in London, the absent scene(s) of the physical end of courtship. The unnarrated physical transformation of Lydia's body "offstage" is implied here in the cataclysmic onset of illness, in sudden corporeal metamorphoses that, like Lydia's loss of virginity, are the effect or end result of strong feeling. Second, this displacement of the physiology of sex is not merely a response to Austen's discreet refusal to narrate Lydia's fall; it also allows Austen to trope the sexual. Lydia's actions initiate a series of corporeal disruptions that associate her sexuality, and sexuality itself, with illness, and it is worth noting that, like illness, the effects of Lydia's sexuality spread through a sort of contagion. On one level this simply reflects the moral "taint" that Lydia's actions cast on her mother and sisters, yet the fact that this "contamination" is physically literalized, moving from body to body, strengthens the analogy to disease. In this context, it does not seem entirely accidental that courtship in the novel begins with illness, with the cold that confines Jane to Netherfield.

The disorder associated with the sexual does not stop here, however. If it causes the females of the Bennet family to fall ill,

Lydia's elopement has a parallel effect on Mr. Bennet. Normally phlegmatic, Mr. Bennet's "excessive distress" at the news suggests to Jane that his state of mind will not allow him to act in "the best and safest way" (276) when he pursues the pair to London. Mrs. Bennet later articulates what is implicit in Jane's remark: "Now here's Mr. Bennet gone away, and I know he will fight Wickham, wherever he meets him, and then he will be killed, and what is to become of us all?" (287). Although Mr. Bennet does not, as it happens, fight Wickham, Mrs. Bennet's fears demonstrate another disruption attendant on Lydia's elopement and suggest additional links between the sexual and disorder.

Despite the fact that a duel with Wickham would be a conventional, and socially regulated, response to Lydia's loss of honor, such an event would nonetheless literally disrupt the social organization, the rules of civility collapsing into violent confrontation. More significantly, however, the event metaphorically extends the scandal of the sexual, implicitly expanding the associations of sexuality and somatic disruption. For the idea of the duel insists that the men involved physically reenact the incident that generates it. If Lydia's sexuality is re-presented internally as illness in the Bennet women, for the men it raises the possibility of a violation imposed on the body from without, a reflex onto the male body of the loss of corporeal and moral "integrity" that Wickham has induced in Lydia. Thus the sexual is also symbolically "contagious" for the male, creating a displaced threat of violent corporeal change that both stems from and re-creates the physical transformation experienced by Lydia.

If the threat of a duel thus serves as an additional re-creation of Lydia's "fall," it also extends Austen's troping of the sexual. Productive of physical violence, at least potentially, sexuality is seen as itself a sort of emotional violence. Although, as Mrs. Gardiner notes, the idea of being "violently in love" is a hackneyed expression that cannot be taken too seriously, the phrase is nonetheless applied to Darcy at the novel's end during his second proposal to Elizabeth, and it thus echoes Darcy's own discussion of the "force of passion" that has swept aside his rational objections to Elizabeth's family when he proposes for the first time. Austen may parody the conventional use of the phrase, but strong emotion in general, and romantic and sexual feeling in particular, are nonetheless associated in the novel with a psychic violence that is both literalized and displaced in Mr. Bennet's "transports of rage" on hearing of Lydia's elopement. Lydia's actions not only raise the possibility of a violent disruption of the social order by linking sexuality, if only indirectly and potentially, to physical violence, but they also uncover Austen's association of the sexual with violent emotion. If the (absent) scene of sexuality is thus linked for Austen with social, corporeal, and emotional disorder, with disease and violence, it is not surprising that Austen does not narrate it directly. As the preceding paragraph suggests, the novel focuses instead on the least physical of the aspects of sexuality: sexual desire. Austen further mutes the sexual in the novel by playing on the contemporary ambiguity of the word *passion,* which could mean strong emotion, ardent love, or sexual feeling. Suggested in courtship situations, sexual desire is finally subsumed under the concept of love, romantic desire. Thus, when Lydia's passions are said to be stronger than her virtue (312), her motives seem obviously sexual to a modern audience, yet Elizabeth and Jane can construe her elopement as evidence that she is "lost to everything but love" of Wickham.[1] Even when it is presented as love, however, filtered through the concept of romantic desire, sexual desire has subtle but dangerous implications in the novel.

The disruptive effects of sexual desire do not appear in physical palpitations or potential duels but unfold instead in an apparently more pleasant context, in Lydia's description of a bit of "fun" at Colonel Forster's: "We dressed up Chamberlayne in woman's clothes, on purpose to pass for a lady,—only think what fun! Not a soul knew of it, but Col. and Mrs. Forster, and Kitty and me, except my aunt, for we were forced to borrow one of her gowns; and you cannot imagine how well he looked! When Denny, and Wickham, and Pratt, and two or three more of the men came in, they did not know him in the least. Lord! how I laughed! and so did Mrs. Forster. I thought I should have died. And *that* made the men suspect something, and then they soon found out what was the matter" (221). Typically, Elizabeth listens "as little as she [can]" to Lydia's narrative. Because it uncovers the hidden dangers of desire in the novel, however, the incident deserves more attention than Elizabeth gives it.

Transmuting male into female, Lydia's joke manipulates one of the basic distinctions on which the social order is based, and this play with gender difference illustrates Marjorie Garber's assertion that transvestite scenes in literature invariably signal a "category crisis," uncovering the instability of cultural boundaries or distinctions and provoking a "crisis of category itself" (1992, 16–17). Garber argues that this crisis is often displaced onto distinctions other than gender difference, and Austen's sense of the dangerous implications of this scene would seem to be focused less on the instability of gender categories than on the transgressive potential of sexual desire. Presented in a courtship setting, Chamberlayne is said to look "well," and for the briefest of moments, there is the chance that one of the officers might be physically attracted to this "lady." Lydia's laughter soon gives the joke away, but the incident nonetheless hints at an implicit assumption, a "truth" that is not universally acknowledged in the novel: sexual desire can ignore society's attempts to regulate or direct it.

In this case, Chamberlayne's attractiveness threatens the heterosexual imperative, implying the possible existence of a homosexual eros that would obliterate what Nancy Armstrong has called "the sexual contract," the organization of Western society since the eighteenth century around a cultural distinction between male and female that is both created by and assured in courtship (1987, 41).[2] What the incident suggests, then, however obliquely or unconsciously, is Austen's sense of sexual desire as not only productive of chaotic effects but as itself disordered, resistant to order. Implicitly presented as polymorphous here, desire, Austen suggests, can disregard any of the fundamental regulations or differences used to order society, such as the cultural distinction between acceptable (heterosexual) and unacceptable (homosexual) object choices; it is equally capable of ignoring class distinctions.[3] In a sense, Lydia's prank is thus a ludic, carnivalesque anticipation of her own elopement, which, by breaking social rules, not only enacts the socially disruptive potential of "passion" but also suggests the deeper scandal of desire for Austen: its potential to create a crisis of categories, to violate the logical foundations—the cultural boundaries and the distinctions and differences—of her society.[4]

Sexuality, in the form of sexual desire, is thus subtly associated in the novel not simply with disorder but also with a principle of "in-difference," with the erasure of social distinctions. As Austen makes clear, such in-difference is inherent in desire in general. Although the novel focuses primarily on the specific romantic desires of the characters, Austen nonetheless hints at a comprehensive theoretical definition of desire during Elizabeth's meditations on her proposed trip with the Gardiners, a point where her desire briefly shifts to a nonromantic object. Initially conceived as a tour of the Lake District, the plan comes for Elizabeth at a time when Bingley's desertion of Jane and Wickham's defection to Miss King have made her cynical about men. She views the trip as a substitute: "Adieu to disappointment and spleen. What are men to rocks and mountains? Oh! what hours of transport we shall spend" (154). As the trip approaches, Elizabeth continues to be enthusiastic, if only because her expectations of pleasure at Wickham's departure from the neighborhood are unfulfilled: "Upon the whole, therefore, she found, what has been sometimes found before, that an event to which she had looked forward with impatient desire, did not in taking place, bring all the satisfaction she had promised herself. It was consequently necessary to name some other period for the commencement of actual felicity; . . . and by again enjoying the pleasure of anticipation, console herself for the present, and prepare for another disappointment. Her tour to the Lakes was now the object of her happiest thoughts" (237).

Concerned with mundane wishes and expectations, the passage nonetheless clarifies the nature of all desire. Beyond its pursuit of any individual object, desire is implicitly defined here as a lack, the absence of satisfaction. As such, desire seeks pleasure; its goal is the commencement of "actual felicity." Austen suggests, however, that pleasure continually eludes us, and desire pursues it through a series of deferrals and displacements. Except for the dubious pleasure of anticipation, gratification is always elsewhere: in the Lake District if not at home, in mountains if not in men, in the future if not in the present. Elizabeth's expectation of pleasure is focused here on the tour, as the pun on "transport" indicates, but the trip is itself an apt metaphor for desire, a journey whose destination—satisfaction—is always a bit further ahead. In fact, Elizabeth's excursion will not fulfill her hopes of delight but will simply produce another displacement, a return to a romantic object. Visiting Pemberley, Elizabeth will come to recognize her desire for Darcy.

As such, Austen's definition of desire anticipates Lacan's in its stress on the impossibility of satisfaction.[5] Of particular significance here is Austen's sense that desire is a process of *glissement,* a continual sliding of interest from object to object. For the *glissement* of desire explains Austen's idea of the in-difference of the sexual, desire's tendency to evade cultural attempts to articulate differences or distinctions. This is not simply because, as we have seen, desire can ignore cultural restrictions on object choice but also because the infinite substitutability of the objects of desire suggests a principle of universal equivalence. If Elizabeth can pursue men *or* mountains in her quest for satisfaction, then all objects are equal in desire's eyes; a hierarchical ordering is impossible. Moreover, because it is theoretically eternal, desire resists boundaries. Continually shifting its attention to a new object once its goal has been obtained, desire is literally boundless, without end. Desire is thus immeasurable and indivisible, incapable of being segmented and ordered. Polymorphous and endless, desire is presented as implicitly antithetical not only to the differences that organize society but also to the idea of difference itself.

It is the infinite substitutability of the objects of desire that most clearly haunts the novel, evidenced, for example, in the continual shifting of Wickham's attentions (from Elizabeth to Miss King to Elizabeth to Lydia) or in the "strangeness" of Mr. Collins making two marriage proposals in a space of three days (125) as he transfers his affections from Jane to Elizabeth to Charlotte Lucas. Lydia, however, best illustrates the principle. As Elizabeth reflects when hearing of the elopement, although she never noticed any partiality for Wickham on Lydia's part, Lydia's affections have illustrated the mutability of desire: "Sometimes one officer, sometimes another had been her favourite, as their attentions raised them in her opinion. Her affections had been continually fluctuating, but never without an object" (280). Elizabeth goes on to lament the "mischief" produced by "mistaken indulgence" to such a temperament, implying that stricter internal or external regulation could restrain the shifting effects of sexual interest. What is concealed in Elizabeth's meditations, however, is the applicability of this description of Lydia to her own case, for Elizabeth's romantic aspirations in the novel also shift: from Wickham to Colonel Fitzwilliam to Darcy, her emotions depending precisely on the extent to which "their attentions raise them in her opinion."

This contradiction suggests an additional difficulty at the core of Austen's novel, a problem beyond Austen's sense of the sexual as dangerously chaotic—namely, the inherent tendency of the sexual to subvert any attempt to represent it. Although Austen would seem to articulate a clear, moralized schema for evaluating romantic attachments in the novel, a closer look suggests that the text's treatment of love and desire collapses into incoherence. Meditating on the growth of Elizabeth's affection for Darcy, the narrator would seem to resolve the problem of making a distinction between the *glissement* of Lydia's affections and those of Elizabeth: "If gratitude and esteem are good foundations of affection, Elizabeth's change of sentiment will be neither improbable nor faulty. But if otherwise, if the regard springing from such sources is unreasonable or unnatural, in comparison of what is so often described as arising on a first interview with its object, and even before two words have been exchanged, nothing can be said in her defence, except that she had given somewhat of a trial to the latter method, in her partiality for Wickham, and that its ill-success might perhaps authorize her to seek the other less interesting mode of attachment" (279). This contrast of "rational" love and love at first sight works not only to distinguish Elizabeth from Lydia but also to distinguish between the objects of Elizabeth's interest, to mark off her true affection for Darcy from her mistaken partiality for Wickham.

The only difficulty is that this doctrine is not entirely borne out by the narrative itself. While it may be true in Elizabeth's case, it hardly applies to Darcy, who, having rejected Elizabeth "at first sight" as not handsome enough, could be said to fall in love on second sight, certainly long before he knows her character or is able to feel gratitude and esteem for her effect on him (23). Similarly, Jane and Bingley, whose marital happiness is never in question, exemplify precisely the workings of that "less interesting mode of attachment." Even filtered through romantic love, sexual desire, it would seem, creates disorder not only within the narrative but also to the narrative, causing the novel's articulations of proper and improper romantic modes, itself an attempt at a hierarchical ordering of desire, to collapse in contradictions.

THE PROBLEM OF SATISFACTION AND THE CONSTRUCTION OF REPRESSION

The sexual thus creates a complex ideological scandal at the heart of *Pride and Prejudice*. Beyond the association of sexuality with disorder, desire is articulated as a complex metonymic process that erases difference and distinctions. Moreover, desire creates particular problems of narrativity, the narrative's representations of the romantic and the sexual collapsing in incoherence. Desire poses another, and even more complicated, narrative problem, however, and Austen's solution to it begins to suggest how the sexual can be both controlled and represented in the novel. This difficulty is, in fact, the problem of how to end the narration. If, in theory, desire is eternal and pleasure always absent, how is the narrative to be resolved? How can desire, and the novel, end? As D. A. Miller has argued, such questions are intrinsic not only to Austen's fiction but to novels in general. Happiness, Miller argues, has no story because it provides nothing to tell; narration depends on a lack, on "insufficiencies, defaults, and deferrals" (1981, 3). In principle, such narratability is limitless, but the marriage plot of the comic novel serves to "name" desire, to provide it with an object choice that allows narrative closure (44–46). *Pride and Prejudice* bears out Miller's argument. Having obtained the object of their romantic desires, Elizabeth and Jane (not to mention Darcy and Bingley) are free from any sort of lack, financial or otherwise. At the novel's end they are provided with a utopian existence whose primary characteristic is the absence of anything to wish for. In addition to "every other source of happiness," the sisters are settled within thirty miles of each other, and their pleasure seems total. Their satisfaction complete, they would seem to be immune not only from desire but from narration.

We are still left with a question, however. How does Austen reconcile the closure of the marriage plot with her sense of the eternal renewal of desire? How have these characters managed to avoid desire's endless *glissement*? The obvious answer is that their final bliss is a reflection of the moral structure of the novel. Elizabeth and Darcy's personal flaws block the fulfillment of their desires. Darcy conceals his love for Elizabeth because of his pride, which is repelled by her social standing and her family's lack of decorum. Elizabeth represses her love for Darcy because her pride has been wounded by his snub. Purged of their pride in the course of the narrative, humbled and matured, they are able to admit their desires directly. Once their love is openly stated during the second marriage proposal, their desires can be satisfied. The characters' final happiness is an indirect reward for their moral growth (Heilman 1975).[6]

Valid for Elizabeth and Darcy, such an interpretation cannot explain the rest of the narrative. Jane and Bingley's romance does not bear out the assumption that the satisfaction of desire is a by-product of moral development. Jane and Bingley are prevented from consummating their love by diffidence, which makes each doubt that his or her love is reciprocated, and they are separated by Bingley's malleability, which makes him excessively dependent on Darcy's opinion. If the lovers eventually achieve complete pleasure, this is not because they have reformed these defects. They continue to be "so complying," as Mr. Bennet jokes, that "nothing will ever be resolved on." Their reunion is brought about, instead, by a reversal of Darcy's machinations, itself evidence that Bingley is still easily influenced. The satisfaction of desire is thus not always the result of moral maturation. Moral growth cannot explain why Elizabeth and Darcy, much less Jane and Bingley, are finally able to avoid desire's theoretical insatiability, its tendency to select another object once its current goal has been obtained.

The satisfaction of desire in *Pride and Prejudice* is not derived, then, from the overt moral structure of the novel. Rather, it follows a more circuitous logic. In effect, satisfaction or pleasure come from their renunciation. Gratification depends finally on an ascesis, on suffering and a renunciation of satisfaction. Elizabeth's sole reservation about her trip with the Gardiners is that Jane will not accompany them, but she concludes that it is fortunate that she has something to wish for: "Were the whole arrangement complete, my disappointment would be certain. But here, by carrying with me one ceaseless source of regret in my sister's absence, I may reasonably hope to have all my expectations of pleasure realized. A scheme of which every part promises delight, can never be successful; and general disappointment is only warded off by the defence of some little peculiar vexation" (237–38). Pleasure, the fulfillment of desire, can never be total. Expecting perfect happiness, Elizabeth would certainly not find satisfaction; a "little peculiar vexation," however, serves magically to ensure gratification. In this case the "source of regret" that guarantees happiness is concurrent—Jane's absence—but in the novel as a whole the principle operates temporally. Absent in the present, pleasure will come in the future; grasped in the present, pleasure will evaporate. Desire, Austen suggests, can be satisfied only after it has been repressed and any expectation of its fulfillment given up. Only when Jane has accepted Bingley's defection does he return and renew his addresses. Only when Elizabeth decides that "connubial felicity" with Darcy is impossible because of Lydia's misalliance does he propose again. If Jane and Bingley or Elizabeth and Darcy finally achieve complete satisfaction, a bliss that marks the end of all desire, this is because they have already suffered.

Desire in the novel is thus governed by an ascetic logic based on an economy of pleasure. Repressing desire and renouncing satisfaction, one experiences the necessary amount of unhappiness. Repression is then magically lifted, one's desire automatically satisfied, the endless *glissement* of desire halted. This principle is confirmed by the negative example of Lydia. Rejecting personal repression or cultural restriction of her desires, Lydia continually seeks immediate, complete gratification. Her "disdain of all restraint," whether internally or externally imposed, leads to her elopement with Wickham, a synecdoche of her tendency to grasp at instant, total pleasure. Having refused to lack anything, however, Lydia ends the novel unsatisfied. Her marriage having sunk into mutual indifference, her income insufficient, Lydia is condemned to eternal want, both romantic and financial. Unrenounced, desire can never be satisfied; avoided, misery becomes eternal. As Elizabeth notes after hearing that the Gardiners have taken Lydia to their home so that she may be married with a modicum of respectability: "If such goodness does not make her miserable now, she will never deserve to be happy" (305). It is because she fails to realize this principle that there can be, finally, no love for Lydia.

It is the curious logic encapsulated in Elizabeth's statement that allows us to understand not only Austen's idea of desire but her concept of sexual repression. Although the novel seems to illustrate perfectly our post-Freudian notions of repression as a (reified) psychic mechanism that controls a preexisting desire, the work should be seen instead as an example of the contemporary definition and institution—the creation—of the concept of repression, the development of the very ideas that will be fully articulated at the end of the century by Freud. As Nancy Armstrong has noted, it is during the eighteenth century that notions of gender are interiorized as subjectivity and a recognizable, modern concept of the self emerges, a process that began with women and was later extended to men. This process moves identity inward, shifting the notion of the self away from one's external familial and kinship relations and from signs of status marked externally through sumptuary display (Armstrong 1987, 3–27; Thompson 1988, 12–13, 106–7).[7] For our purposes, the crucial aspect of this shift is the parallel migration of the sexual, the eighteenth-century reconceptualization of sexuality. No longer conceived merely as a series of external actions, the sexual is now internalized, seen as the desires and sexual impulses of the self (Foucault 1978, 19–20).

This implantation of the sexual within the individual is accompanied by the development of a corresponding idea of self-restraint: sexual repression. If the creation of the idea of an interiorized self is usually linked to the rise of a bourgeois stress on the individual, an additional effect of emerging capitalism is the internalization of the doctrine of deferred gratification, the basis for the accumulation of capital. Translated from an economic doctrine to a moral one, deferred gratification becomes an insistence on self-control, including, particularly for women, an insistence on modesty and chastity, on sexual self-regulation (Poovey 1984, 10, 27; Armstrong 1987, 81).[8] As such, the notion of an economy of pleasure presented in *Pride and Prejudice* can be seen as an additional transcription of the doctrine of deferred gratification, which is presented in the novel not only as a moral imperative but also as a psychological "reality," as the unfolding of a set of psychological principles. If the concept of a limited amount of pleasure, which must be deferred to be fully enjoyed, is presented in the novel as a universal "law," this law is fully internalized, enacted within and by the characters. The gratification of desire is thus not only seen morally, as a reward, but also conceived as an inevitable result, as the necessary effect of self-regulation.

As the psychologized reflex of an economic doctrine, sexual repression is thus not an inherent psychic mechanism but a construction that brings into focus the notion of the self where it is supposed to inhere. As Armstrong notes of the Victorian novel, the idea of repression, embodied in various characters, is less the product of the characters' psychology than precisely the means of creating the idea of the inner depths of the self (1987, 165). By the same token, the idea of repression also articulates the concept of desire to which it is opposed. In effect, what Austen presents is the contemporary tendency to interiorize the opposition between culture and nature, between civilized restraint and "wild" behavior. As such, desire and the repression of desire can be seen as mutually creating concepts: a principle of self-regulation is justified by contrast to an idea of unrestrained energy, just as this energy is identified by the regulation intended to control it.

This creation of the notion of repressed desire, of an internalized desire and an interior repressive mechanism, is important not simply because it illustrates the creation of ideas that become fully naturalized in the Victorian novel. In the context of *Pride and Prejudice* itself, the idea of repressed desire serves a vital function, resolving the problems posed by Austen's (corresponding) notion of unrestrained desire. If "repression" is conceived as the containment of desire, the *idea* of repression allows Austen to imagine limits to the idea of chaotic desire constructed in relation to it. Repression, Austen suggests, not only contains desire but transforms it. As Darcy's courtship of Elizabeth demonstrates, Austen implicitly argues that repressed desire focuses on a specific object, and the endless progression of desire from object to object is converted into a movement through symbolic expressions of desire for the same object. As I have argued elsewhere, the novel details Darcy's repeated symbolic expressions of sexual interest in Elizabeth through glances and proposals to dance or to walk (Allen 1985, 426–34).[9] As such, repression realigns desire with the principle of difference, with a discrimination among the objects of desire. Repressed, Darcy's desire is rendered hierarchical, so that some objects become more important than others. Elizabeth is Darcy's actual goal, and his demands for dances and walks are merely a pursuit of secondary symbolic pleasures. Moreover, repression also halts both the *glissement* of desire itself and the "contagion," the metonymic illness and violence, it produces. Repression replaces the erratic metonymies of desire with a controlled metonymy: the displacement of desire into a series of symbolic demands that allow the indirect expression of one's desire for a particular object. As a result, repression also solves the problem of the potential endlessness of desire's metonymies. Because it focuses on a specific object, repressed desire is provided with a boundary. The attainment of the object—marriage to a

Darcy or an Elizabeth—ends desire and inaugurates the reign of complete satisfaction.

If Austen thus advocates the repression of desire for her characters as a means of transforming the chaotic indifference of the sexual, this doctrine begins to suggest how the novel itself deals with the disorder associated with desire. In fact, Austen's novel illustrates an early articulation of the strategies used for minimizing the disruptive effects of the sexual in Victorian fiction; in effect, the novel anticipates the Victorian construction of novelistic discretion. I have already noted two techniques that will recur in the Victorian novel. The first strategy is Austen's subordination of the sexual to an idea of romantic love. This stress on romantic love rather than the explicit presentation of sexual attraction is not simply an attempt to conceal sexual desire, however. Rather, it allows Austen to recode the sexual, transforming the universality of biological drives into a private, preordained romantic affinity such as Darcy's love for Elizabeth. Re-presenting desire as an "inevitable" personal tie, Austen is able to mask sexuality's polymorphous impulses. Thus the narrator can assert, for example, that Elizabeth's heart has only been "slightly touched" by Wickham, less because this is supported by the narrative than because the ideology of romantic love implies that she is destined for Darcy. This recoding of the sexual also allows Austen to rewrite the endless movement of desire. The ideology of romantic love insists that "two 'one and onlys' " will find each other out, that romantic desire will "recognize its 'proper object' " (Miller 1981, 96). As such, the shiftings of desire experienced by the characters can be minimized and contained, seen finally as only individual errors: the "imaginary attachments" of Mr. Collins or Elizabeth's "mistaken partiality" for Wickham.

The second strategy also serves to minimize the impact of sex and sexuality in the novel, although in a far more obvious fashion: Austen simply refuses to narrate the sexual directly. Thus the sexual action of the novel, Lydia's elopement, takes place "offstage." The workings of this device are obvious; by consigning sexuality to the periphery of the narrative, Austen is able to forestall a full recognition of its chaotic implications. Moreover, Austen is also able to avoid the additional problems posed by the actual ineffability of the sexual, eliding both the difficulty of defining it and its tendency to disrupt any attempt to represent it (although, as we have seen, she does not entirely escape the latter problem). Sexuality, however, is not banished from the novel. In fact, the absent scene(s) of Lydia's cohabitation are crucial to the work as a negative example to the other characters and the reader, as an impediment to the union of Darcy and Elizabeth, and as a source of narrative interest and tension. As D. A. Miller has noted, if the ideology of Austen's work insists on "settlement," on the institution of order and the discovery of truth, the very existence of the narrative itself depends on precisely the opposite qualities—on uncertainty, confusion, and disorder (1981, 50–54).

As such, Lydia's elopement anticipates a common pattern in the Victorian novel, which often revolves around a sexual scene that is not itself narrated. *Pride and Prejudice* thus anticipates the dilemma of representing sex and sexuality in Victorian fiction. Associated with the chaotic, the sexual cannot be directly represented in the novel, yet it is impossible to ignore. Thus Austen's rather Senecan approach to the sexual—her siting of the sexual action of the novel behind the scenes—resolves this difficulty and establishes a strategy deployed by the novels that follow *Pride and Prejudice,* namely, direct presentation of the sexual is replaced by techniques for representing sexual material indirectly. The function of such techniques is not simply to reduce the anxiety produced by the sexual, controlling the disorder associated with sex and sexuality. Such strategies also address the actual ineffability of the sexual by producing and defining it in ways that make its representation possible. In *Pride and Prejudice,* Austen focuses on two such techniques whose workings have already been suggested by the novel's content: a complex representation of the body, and the submission of the sexual to a symbolic calculus.

Of the two, Austen's treatment of the body is more obvious. If Austen rejects the doctrine of love at first sight, this is because it places too much emphasis on the purely physical. Beyond or behind the "rational" objections to such a mode of falling in love, however, lies a deeper difficulty: Austen's sense that the body is the locus of (the disorders of) sexuality (Tanner 1986, 132). As a result, Austen minimizes the body in the narrative, a strategy apparent in descriptions such as the introduction of Darcy and Bingley: "Mr. Bingley was good looking and gentlemanlike; he had a pleasant countenance, and easy, unaffected manners. . . . but his friend Mr. Darcy soon drew the attention of the room by his fine, tall person, handsome features, noble mien; and the report . . . of his having ten thousand a year" (10). These are some of the most complete physical descriptions in the novel; the Bennet girls, for example, are never described by the narrator at all, and Mr. Collins is presented as "a tall, heavy looking young man of five and twenty. His air was grave and stately, and his manners were very formal" (64). What is immediately apparent is the paucity and generality of physical description and the almost immediate shift to other concerns: income, in Darcy's case, and, more often, manners and social self-presentation, such as Bingley's easy ways or Collins's grave and stately air. In fact, Austen suggests, physical attractiveness is interpretive, influenced by other perceptions. Thus Darcy's manners are sufficiently unpleasant that they lead to a public re-vision of his appearance. Appalled by his pride, the assembly at Meryton soon decides that Darcy has a "forbidding, disagreeable countenance."

Such a suppression of the body, while it shifts attention from the physical to the moral, is balanced by a continual return of the body in the novel, however. In addition to the emphasis on the corporeal, on illness and violence, that both follows and represents Lydia's elopement, the body suppressed in introductory descriptions is re-presented indirectly throughout the narrative, recurring as the site of emotion. This is evident in the continual references to the blushes that signal Elizabeth's and Jane's feelings for Darcy and Bingley, but it is clearest in a less significant incident, the Gardiner children's response to their parents' return: "When the carriage drove up to the door, the joyful surprise that lighted up their faces, and displayed itself over their whole bodies, in a variety of capers and frisks, was the first pleasing earnest of their welcome" (286). It is appropriate that it is the "little Gardiners" who most clearly demonstrate the reintroduction of the body into the narrative, for the technique is precisely an attempt to render the body innocent. What Austen does by minimizing physical description and then reinscribing the body in this way is to substitute the semiotic body, the body as sign of emotion, for the sexual body, which creates emotion. In other words, Austen virtually erases the body as the source of desire, as the physical cause of romantic and sexual attraction, and repositions it as the sign of desire's effects.

This technique works both to repress the chaotic aspects of the sexual and to produce the sexual by defining it in ways that make its representation possible. If the erasure of the sexual body mystifies the origins of sexual desire and minimizes the physical component of romantic attraction, this erasure replaces the body that produces the disorder of sexual attraction with a body that generates the order of rational analysis. Although the signs of emotion, written on the body, still cannot be completely controlled, as Elizabeth's involuntary "heightenings of color" suggest, yet the chaos of the sexual is transformed here because desire is translated into the signs of desire, implicitly submitted to, and controlled by, interpretation. Moreover, rather than serving as the cause of (unrepresentable) sexual feeling, the body thus becomes synonymous with meaning itself, with the physical symptoms that act as signs of emotion. Reduced to the somatic display of its effects, the sexual is thus aligned with the possibility of representation.[10]

Austen's recuperation of the body in order to contain the disorder of the sexual and to make possible its representation is paralleled by a reworking of desire itself. We have already seen how an ethic of deferred gratification applied to the characters transforms desire, and a similar technique operates at the narrative level both to control and to represent sexual feeling. As it happens, this strategy is clearest at the point where it is furthest from sexual desire: in the personality of Mr. Collins. When Elizabeth visits the Collinses at Hunsford, one of the first evidences of Mr. Collins's hospitality is his tour of the grounds of the parsonage, where he points out the views from his garden "with a minuteness which left beauty entirely behind. He could number the fields in every direction, and could tell how many trees there were in the most distant clump" (156). Unfortunately, the ladies are not properly clad to explore Collins's "two meadows," but the tour continues the next day, when the party is invited to Rosings, where Mr. Collins "enumerates the windows in the front of the house" and relates the cost of their glazing (161).

Such behavior is perfectly typical for Collins, a reflection of his bourgeois tendency to fix and define social differences through the description and quantification of material possessions (Baudrillard 1981, 29–62). As Elizabeth's displeased reactions clearly indicate, such materialism is to be seen as vulgar. Even if Elizabeth's responses to Pemberley did not perform a parallel operation, however (the evaluation not of Darcy's social status but of his taste and character through an assessment of his possessions), the entire novel is imbued with similar manifestations of the emergent ideology of capitalism: the insistence of both characters and narrator on the value of quantification. If Collins's enumeration of the views is said to leave beauty behind, the same principle is nonetheless invoked precisely to assess Jane's attractiveness. After the ball where Jane meets Bingley, Elizabeth notes that Jane was "five times as pretty as every other woman in the room," and Bingley's cognizance of this fact is implied by his having asked her to dance a second time. If, on one level, Elizabeth's remark simply represents the effusions of sisterly affection, it also suggests how Austen deals with the chaotic indifference and the unrepresentability of the sexual.

As Roland Barthes has noted, beauty cannot really be explained. As an abstraction, it is "mute," and it can be articulated only through a catalog of attributes that is always incomplete, potentially endless, or through tautology ("she was beautiful") and comparisons ("as beautiful as . . ."), which simply displace the problem (Barthes 1974, 33, 114). By combining these techniques, however, Austen suggests a solution to the problem. Because the sexual body that is the locus of beauty is erased in the text, Austen replaces the blazon that enumerates beauty's attributes with the quantification implicit in such a catalog. Thus, Jane's beauty is not described but simply indicated through a numerical comparison ("five times as pretty"). While this does not actually define the beautiful (which, as we have seen, must be minimized in the novel in any case), it nonetheless allows the representation of the otherwise unrepresentable. Quantified and numerically fixed, the otherwise unstateable can be articulated.

This use of quantification performs a crucial function in the novel, for it also allows Austen to define and represent sexual desire, which, as abstract sensation and emotion, creates similar difficulties of representation. The process is best summarized by Elizabeth's conversation with Mrs. Gardiner about Bingley's being "violently in love" with Jane. As Mrs. Gardiner notes, this expression is "so doubtful, so indefinite" that it gives her little idea of Bingley's feelings, especially since, vague in itself, the phrase is as often used to describe the result of a "half-hour's acquaintance" as a "real, strong attachment." Elizabeth responds by recasting the terms of the definition: "I never saw a more promising inclination. He was growing quite inattentive to other people, and wholly engrossed by her. Every time they met, it was more decided and remarkable. At his own ball he offended two or three young ladies, by not asking them to dance, and I spoke to him twice myself, without receiving an answer" (141). If Elizabeth begins here by jokingly defining romantic interest as a "general incivility" to everyone else, her assessment is finally given form by counting the ladies slighted or the number of times Bingley was "uncivil" to her. As such, the passage replicates Elizabeth's earlier conversation with Charlotte Lucas, where Jane and Bingley's relationship, the extent of Jane's possible attraction to Bingley, is determined through a minute enumeration of their interactions. Jane cannot fully know the extent of her own regard, Elizabeth argues, because she has only "danced four dances with him at Meryton; she saw him one morning at his own house, and has since dined in company with him four times" (22). Mrs. Bennet is not the only character who assesses romantic interest by counting proposals to dance.

The continual tendency of both characters and narrator to quantify the signs of romantic (and hence, implicitly, sexual) attraction constrains the disorder associated with the sexual. Through quantification, the amorphous, unending qualities of sexuality and desire are submitted to a symbolic ordering, which reduces sexual anxiety by bounding desire mathematically. This is clearest, as one might suspect, in the negative example of Lydia, emerging in her anticipations of pleasure in her forthcoming visit with the Forsters: "In Lydia's imagination, a visit to Brighton comprised every possibility of earthly happiness. She saw with the creative eye of fancy, the streets of that gay bathing place covered with officers. She saw herself the object of attention, to tens and to scores of them at present unknown. She saw all the glories of the camp; its tents stretched forth in beauteous uniformity of lines, crowded with the young and the gay, and dazzling with scarlet; and to complete the view, she saw herself seated beneath a tent, tenderly flirting with at least six officers at once" (232). In effect, Lydia's vision is a summary of sexual chaos, the chaos of the sexual, for it aligns a vision of the virtually unquantifiable with undifferentiated desire, the polymorphous attraction to six or tens or scores of officers. And the passage itself performs, in miniature, the operation of quantification carried on in the narrative at large. If the first three sentences seem typical of Lydia, the final sentence seems more appropriate to the narrator, not only because Lydia does not seem the type to find any sort of "uniformity" to be "beauteous," but also because the vision of flirtation is curiously narrowed from streets covered with officers to a mere six men in a tent. If Lydia's tendency to indiscriminate sexuality is articulated through a vision of the (almost) uncountable, the general tendency of characters and narrator to bound and contain sexual desire through enumeration is suggested by the fixing of Lydia's desire on a particular (although still clearly excessive) number of officers.

Beyond its uses as an additional check to the chaotic indifference of the sexual, quantification also makes possible the represention of sexual desire. As Elizabeth's reply to Mrs. Gardiner's remark suggests, quantification gives a definite, measurable form to the otherwise indefinite. As such, a final function of Austen's insistence on the repression of desire thus becomes clear. Because repression leads to repetition in the novel—both of a series of symbolic expressions of desire (dances, looks, walks) and of a particular symbolic demand—desire becomes measurable. Thus, for example, if Darcy initially refuses Bingley's suggestion that he dance with Elizabeth, his growing interest in her is signaled by the fact that he marks subsequent encounters by asking her to dance: at Longbourn, at Netherfield during Jane's illness, and at the Netherfield ball. Segmented into repeated actions that can be quantified (three proposals to dance), Darcy's desire can be both systematically gauged and represented. Quantified and enumerated, sexual desire can be submitted to a precise articulation, the ineffability of abstract sensation provided with a definition.

NARRATIVE INTERIORS

Austen thus anticipates the treatment of sex and sexuality in the Victorian novel, reacting to her perception of the disorder associated with the sexual and to its tendency to disrupt representation by employing a variety of techniques intended less to erase the sexual than to bound it and to produce it, to align it with the possibility of representation. In effect, Austen demonstrates the construction of sexual repression not only for the characters but for the novel as well. This idea of the novel as repressed, however, must not be simply understood as an erasure of the sexual in fiction. Rather, it must be seen as a process that, in fact, constitutes the narrative. Just as sexual repression creates a sense of hidden depths in the characters, Austen's sexual reticence, her narrative repression, creates a sense of the interiority of the narrative, of hidden forces and meanings that cannot be directly spoken. As Foucault suggests, the implantation of the sexual in the individual, the shifting of the definition of sexuality from external actions to inner desires, induces a parallel reconceptualization of literature, which is now seen less as a recounting of events than as the attempt to articulate a truth that is hidden "between the words," in the depths of the fiction (1978, 59).

In the Victorian novel as in Austen, I will argue, this "truth" is always tautologically linked in some way to the sexual, which, unspoken on the "surface" of the narrative, creates the sense of a narrative interior. This produces the central paradox of the representation of sex and sexuality in Victorian fiction. The nineteenth-century novel must always seek to speak the sexual "truth," but this "truth" cannot be directly spoken. This is not only because, as we have seen, the sexual is linked to the chaotic or because it is intrinsically unrepresentable, disrupting attempts to textualize it. Finally, the direct representation of the sexual would empty the text of meaning, for the text's significance, its "truth," depends precisely on a sense that "truth" remains hidden. Conversely, however, the sexual cannot be completely erased from the text. For the narrative to prove satisfactory, the sexual "truth" at its core must at least be intimated, the promise of "meaning" held out to the reader. If, as Brontë insists, Austen rejects a "speaking acquaintance" with desire, if *Pride and Prejudice* only speaks desire indirectly, this may not be because the passions are unknown to her but because she understands them all too well.

In the authors who follow Austen, both this erotic understanding and its indirect expression become increasingly complex. As I argue in the next chapter, Elizabeth Gaskell simultaneously satirizes and enacts the doctrine of sexual repression in her analysis of the relation between biological "facts" and cultural codes. Moreover, investigating contemporary ideas of gender difference, Gaskell uncovers some of the problematic implications of the erotic discretion advocated by Austen—specifically, the difficulty of defining gender difference if such discretion involves a narrative suppression of the (gendered) body. Gaskell's solutions to these problems illustrate the growing sophistication of Victorian representations of sex and sexuality at midcentury. If Austen demonstrates the cultural construction of such concepts as *sexual desire* and *repression,* Gaskell, as we shall see, goes a step further, finding the possibility of sexual representation less in a rejection of "nature" than in the manipulation of the fictions of "culture."

CHAPTER 3

"Peter Was a Lady Then":
Sexuality and Gender in *Cranford*

In the first place, if the town of Cranford is "in possession of the Amazons," *Cranford,* the novel in which it appears, may be in the possession of the feminists. Ever since Martin Dodsworth's charge that the novel expiates Elizabeth Gaskell's unconscious hostility to men through a recognition of the insufficiency of women (1963, 132–45), women readers have exercised their right to re-vision. For Elaine Showalter, the novel "is probably an Amazon utopia" set in the "wild zone" of women's experience outside the control of male-dominated society (1981, 201). Similarly, Patricia Wolfe argues that the novel is based on a repudiation of patriarchal values, evident in the town's movement away from Deborah Jenkyns's emphasis on a rigid code of social rules introjected from the father and the substitution of Miss Matty as a model of maternal love and kindness. The novel thus rejects a "perverted feminism" based on masculine models in favor of a "natural appreciation of femininity" (1968, 161–76). Nina Auerbach agrees, stressing Gaskell's portrayal of the triumph of the values of a community of women over those of the male "warrior world" of the nearby industrial town of Drumble (1978, 87). As a result, Rowena Fowler asserts, the novel solves a perennial problem in fiction by depicting strong women who are still women, not mere imitators of male aggression (1984, 717–29).

What is initially striking about these commentaries is that they fall into two gendered interpretive camps. For Dodsworth, whether one considers the characters or the author, a woman must admit her inadequacy and resubmit to a male authority, just as Peter takes control of Matty's life or Dodsworth himself steps in as Gaskell's interpreter. If Dodsworth's reading of the work evinces a certain male anxiety about female power, however, women readers of the novel seem equally (although more subtly) combative, determined to show the inadequacy of masculine values, codes of behavior, or modes of interaction. Whether construed as Amazons or "feminine-ists," the women of Cranford emerge triumphant in these readings, having replaced the patriarchy with a new order. Criticism of *Cranford,* then, bears a strong resemblance to the novel itself, with the book, like the town, serving as a battleground for competing masculine and feminine perspectives. In fact, this controversy can be seen as an attempt to establish the gender allegiance of the novel itself. Is *Cranford* male or female? An assertion of the necessity of male dominance or a triumphant presentation of the superiority of strong women?

In one sense these questions cannot be answered. Like the critical positions that give rise to them, they are based on the assumption of the irreducible reality of gender difference: as opposed positions that must battle it out until one subdues the other, or as sets of innate or learned qualities that act as "natural" oppositions, or as the very concept that the genders are inherently different in the first place. As Judith Butler has recently argued, however, gender is not a transcendental reality but only a reflection of socially mandated ideals. Thus notions of both an inner, gendered identity and of gender itself are illusions derived from a culturally determined "performance" of gender that is displayed on and through the body. Thus, Butler argues, "words, acts, gestures, and desire produce the effect of an internal cure or substance, but produce this on the surface of the body" (1990, 136).[1] For Butler, gender is only this performance, a conceptual position that was unavailable to Gaskell. Yet *Cranford* does seem to call Victorian notions of gender into question precisely by problematizing the characters' performances of gender. In a novel in which Deborah Jenkyns is noted for her "masculine" ways and in which her brother Peter's pranks seem to consist largely of dressing up as a lady, Victorian conceptions both of the content of the ideas of "male" and "female" and of an irreducible difference between the genders become entirely problematic. Rather than presenting an argument for the natural superiority of men or women, *Cranford* finally interrogates Victorian assumptions about gender and gender difference. This examination of gender is not an end in itself, however. Gaskell's attempt to find the "real" basis for gender difference both derives from and is used to resolve a larger difficulty: the instability of Victorian conceptions of "culture" and "nature," of the opposition of biological "realities" and cultural codes. As we shall see, this instability is most apparent in relation to Victorian ideas of sex and sexuality.

CULTURAL CODES AND THE VULGAR FACTS

Whether Cranford is an Amazon utopia or not, it is a highly coded one, the Cranford ladies' complex system of taboos and exclusions illustrating an extreme version of nineteenth-century distinctions between "culture" or "civilization" and "nature." Defined politically or anthropologically as the difference between "civilized" England and the "savage" nations and psychologically as an internal division of the individual between rational self-control and instinctual impulses, the Victorian distinction between "culture" and "nature" is defined, in the social realm, as the difference between an idea of the "biological," seen as the facts of the body or the natural world, and notions of "polite" or "refined" behavior. Focused on the town's social codes, Gaskell's presentation of Cranford anatomizes this dichotomy between the biological and the genteel.

One of the defining characteristics of the Cranford ladies is their determination to ignore the "vulgar facts." The expression is introduced in the novel to refer to poverty, the limitation of means that the women of Cranford disguise with the notion that economy is "elegant," but the phrase soon expands to include virtually all of the meanings subsumed under the idea of the "natural." On the most general level, the vulgar facts are those physical realities that must be denied in order to distinguish "culture" from "nature." Thus, the Cranford ladies continually attempt to institute a sort of counternature, apparent in the newspapers placed on new carpeting to protect it from the sun or in Betty Barker's dressing her cow in gray flannel after its fall into a lime pit. The basic principle here—the act of covering to provide protection from nature or to conceal nature or both—is in fact a concrete manifestation of the intrinsic rationale of Cranford's rules of gentility, which also serve, on a more abstract level, to conceal or protect against the biological. If the narrator, Mary Smith, devotes several pages to the "rules and regulations" of mealtime in the Jenkyns household, this is in part because dining is the Cranford ladies' closest contact with "biology," and the experience must be heavily coded precisely to block awareness of the biological realities—the digestive processes, the "natural" origins of the food—that it invokes. In the Jenkyns household, such coding is often taken to extremes: "When oranges came in, a curious proceeding was gone through. Miss Jenkyns did not like to cut the fruit; for, as she observed, the juice all ran out nobody knew where; sucking (only I think she used some more recondite word) was in fact the only way of enjoying oranges; but then there was the unpleasant association with a ceremony frequently gone through by little babies; and so, after dessert, in orange season, Miss Jenkyns and Miss Matty used to rise up, possess themselves each of an orange in silence, and withdraw to the privacy of their own rooms, to indulge in sucking oranges" (Gaskell [1851–53] 1976, 66). Oranges receive so much attention here because they represent food in its natural state, unmediated by the transformations of the kitchen, and because of their associations with natural nourishment—that sucking activity performed by babies, which must itself be renamed and transformed into a "ceremony." As such, sucking oranges must take place outside of "culture" (in silence, in private), lest it disrupt the pretensions of culture.

Dining room etiquette in Cranford, however, does more than serve to establish a civilized "reality" divorced from the physical and the biological. Although the problematic fruit here is the orange and not the apple, Victorian reworkings of the Adam and Eve story equated eating with the indulgence of the sexual appetite (Michie 1987, 15–23), a connection that is hinted at in Miss Jenkyns's association of fruit with babies. Thus Cranford's dining codes serve not only to restrain awareness of the biological in general but to provide a symbolic regulation of the sexual in particular. Both such regulation and its indirect workings are entirely apt, for the most rigorously tabooed subject in Cranford, the most vulgar of the facts, would seem to be sexual matters. Men, the Cranford ladies have persuaded themselves, are "vulgar" by definition, and although Miss Matty's "mysterious dread of men and matrimony" (64) is more extreme than that of the other Cranford women, it is nonetheless fairly typical.

As Matty's encounter with Holbrook after a thirty-year separation suggests, the Cranford ladies' claim that they would rather
live without men is not entirely genuine, yet the incident suggests
how rigorously sexuality is denied in Cranford. The point is not
simply that Matty originally renounced her love for Holbrook
because her father and sister deemed it socially unacceptable but
that, even after seeing Holbrook again, Matty does not speak of
the matter. Informed by Miss Pole of the original story, Mary
Smith instead deduces that Matty retains her love for Holbrook,
that her "poor heart" has been faithful in "its sorrow and its
silence" (78). The repression at work here is, in effect, a double
one. Not only, as in *Pride and Prejudice,* does the notion of love
subsume and conceal the more threatening specter of sexual desire, but love itself is seen as a violation of Cranford's rules of
"feminine decorum." Thus the sexual is doubly distanced. Even if
the Cranford ladies can, at times, bring themselves to speak about
love, they rarely even allude to sex; their sexual anxiety is displaced into domestic surveillance, concern about the romantic
lives of their maidservants, and provides the subtext for the Panic,
the period of fear of burglars and male intruders. No wonder,
then, that Matty evinces an extreme sexual ignorance. It is entirely characteristic that after the marriage of her servant Martha,
Miss Matty remains completely unaware of Martha's pregnancy
until she is presented with the baby.

Virtually oblivious to the "facts of life," Miss Matty is an
extreme yet apt example of Cranford's denial of the sexual. Unlike
dining room etiquette, however, the repression of sex and sexuality in Cranford does not serve merely to establish and enforce a
civilized decorum juxtaposed to the facts of the body. Ultimately,
the suppression of sexuality serves a more basic function: the
maintenance of the social taxonomy itself. As I suggested in chapter 1, Victorian perceptions of class difference are bolstered by
the implicit assumption that they are not arbitrary social constructs but reflections of natural—in fact ontological—distinctions. Gaskell underscores this assumption when Lady Glenmire
arrives in Cranford. Offended by Mrs. Jamieson's snobbish request that they not call on her while Lady Glenmire is visiting, the
Cranford ladies turn their backs on the pair in church, although
they are exceedingly curious about "my lady." Since Matty's servant Martha, however, does not "belong to a sphere of society

whose observation could be an implied compliment" to Lady Glenmire, Matty and Miss Pole are able to grill Martha on the new arrival's appearance. As Martha says:

> "I'll tell you what, ma'am, she's more like Mrs. Deacon, at the 'Coach and Horses,' nor any one."
> "Hush, Martha!" said Miss Matty, "that's not respectful."
> "Isn't it, ma'am? I beg pardon, I'm sure; but Jem Hearn said so as well. He said, she was just such a sharp, stirring sort of a body"—
> "Lady," said Miss Pole.
> "Lady—as Mrs. Deacon." (117-18)

Martha's democratic inability to understand that aristocrats and innkeepers cannot be physically similar is underlined by the interchangeability, for her, of "bodies" and "ladies." In contrast, the women of Cranford are not entirely convinced that ladies have bodies at all, or at least the same sort as other people. They are not certain, for example, that the peerage eat preserves. As such, sexuality is particularly threatening to the social order because, as Matty's youthful romance with Holbrook suggests, it can bring together the rector's daughter and the farmer, suggesting the universality of biology and revealing the artificiality of class distinctions. Ultimately, the repression of the sexual is crucial to the maintenance of the social order because it preserves the middle-class fiction of the ontological basis of class difference, the "natural" difference between bodies and ladies.

Gaskell presents the novel as a gentle satire on the beliefs of the Cranford ladies, continually demonstrating the untenability of some of the ideas that ground Cranford society. In fact, much of the plot of *Cranford* derives from the continual collapse of Cranford's cultural rules when confronted by the biological, especially in the form of sexuality.[2] Thus, when Miss Jessie Brown is left alone in the world by the deaths of her father and sister, Deborah suspends her insistence on "feminine decorum" and allows Miss Jessie to be courted by Major Gordon in the Jenkyns's parlor. Deborah's response here is a practical one—Miss Jessie must find someone to provide for her—but it also implies that Cranford's propriety is artificial, that it must give way before the existence of love and physical attraction. Although Miss Matty is shocked and terrified to discover Major Gordon in the drawing room with his arm around Miss Jessie's waist, the subsequent death of Holbrook makes Matty herself realize the price of sexual repression, the limitation of possibilities imposed on her by her father and sister's snobbish suppression of her romance. Submitting to "fate and love," Matty allows Martha to take Jem Hearn as a "follower."

The return of sexuality, however, does not merely serve to satirize the artificiality of Cranford's codes of sexual decorum. It also demonstrates the arbitrary and tenuous nature of the class differences that constitute Cranford's social structure, a point best exemplified by the progress of Lady Glenmire. Despite Cranford's uncertainty about the matter, Lady Glenmire is not, it turns out, ontologically different from members of the other social classes, a fact she demonstrates during her first meeting with the Cranford ladies by proposing more bread and butter at tea. As Mary Smith realizes, this "mutual want" makes them "better acquainted with her than we should ever have been with talking about the Court" (124). Having begun by revealing that the peerage do in fact eat preserves, Lady Glenmire goes on to prove that aristocrats are biological creatures by becoming engaged to Mr. Hoggins, the local doctor who serves as the epitome of vulgarity for the women of Cranford. Appearing in church with a renewed "flush of youth" in her face and her lips "redder and more trembling full" than before, Lady Glenmire's corporeal existence is hard to deny. Lady Glenmire's engagement thus shatters a number of assumptions on which Cranford society is based, revealing that the notion of an ontological difference between the social classes and the ideal of aristocratic *aphanisis* are fantasies. At the deepest level, Lady Glenmire's demonstration of the universality of sexuality calls into question the taxonomic premises on which the class structure is based.

As one would expect, the Cranford ladies resist contemplating these implications too closely; their initial response to the engagement is to regard it "in the same light as the Queen of Spain's legs—facts which certainly existed, but the less said about the better" (169). Although Gaskell satirizes such beliefs, which ground not only Cranford but also Victorian society, the novel suggests that Gaskell herself is equally, if more subtly, infected by the sexual attitudes that she critiques. Mocking the codes of gentility, Gaskell nonetheless retains the sexual anxiety at their core. This leads to Gaskell's own erasures and elisions of sex and sexuality in the novel. If the novel itself is based on the repeated collision of Cranford's genteel codes with the realities of sexuality, the sexual is nonetheless presented in the novel in heavily mediated forms. The sexual scenes that deflate Cranford's gentility are not only relatively innocent (Major Gordon with his arm around Miss Jessie, Martha kissing Jem Hearn) but distanced in a variety of ways: rather than being directly narrated, they are reported by a character, and this report more often infers the sexual than witnesses it. Thus the kiss between Martha and Jem is represented by Matty's announcement that she hears a noise that "sounds like kissing." Satirizing the Cranford ladies' sexual repression, *Cranford* itself is only slightly less genteel.

This gentility is further evidenced by the novel's own erasure of the facts of the body, the reduction of physical description of the characters to a bare minimum. Helena Michie has noted that narrative description of women in Victorian fiction invokes several codes: clichéd language, the use of synecdoche, and the "meta-trope," the comparison of the character to a work of art or a text. The function of such codes, Michie argues, is to distance female characters and to restrain their physicality, to "capture" or "frame" women (1987, 79–123). The application of such techniques to characters of both genders in *Cranford* and in other Victorian novels, however, suggests that the function of such descriptions is not—or not only—to insist on patriarchal control of women but also to erase the threat presented by the sexual body in general. This is evident from the paradoxes produced by the use of such codes in *Cranford*. Miss Jessie Brown is described exclusively in terms of her childlike face, a synecdoche (the face substituting for the entire body) that is itself further condensed in another synec-doche: the dimples that so offend the Cranford ladies, who insist that it is time Miss Jessie stop "trying to look like a child" (44). It is curious, then, that Mary Smith later notes that, as Mrs. Gordon, Miss Jessie's dimples will not be "out of place." The contra-diction here uncovers a multiple erasure of the body; not only is the sexual body concealed in a series of synecdoches, but the dimples, the sign of Miss Jessie's sexual attractiveness, are them-selves recoded, read as the representation of an opposite meaning: Miss Jessie's (sexual) immaturity.

A similar process governs the narrative presentation of Hol-brook. When he reencounters Miss Matty, he is described as a "tall, thin, Don Quixote-looking old man" (70). In this case, the description is expanded by depicting Holbrook's clothes ("[He] wore a blue coat with brass buttons, drab breeches, and gaiters"), a technique that establishes a physical presence without invoking the body, but the focus of the passage is on the resemblance to Quixote. The reference serves not only to dematerialize, through comparison to a fictional text, the body it purports to invoke but also to introduce a useful semiotic instability. Once again, the description produces a contradiction. Mary Smith eventually decides that the resemblance to Quixote is "only external"; three pages later, however, she insists that the strangeness of Holbrook's behavior makes him "very like Don Quixote" (76). As with Miss Jessie, this contradiction signals a rewriting of the sexual body. Holbrook's inscription as Quixote simultaneously suggests his role as Miss Matty's potential romantic hero and labels this possibility as precisely quixotic; he is far too old, Mary Smith concludes, to fulfill a romantic fantasy. If Holbrook nonetheless begins to court Miss Matty, the comparison also introduces a muted uncertainty about his sanity that further qualifies Holbrook's suitability for, and the possibility of, romance. Thus, even before Holbrook's death removes the hope of a romantic (and presumably sexual) relation for Miss Matty, narrative description denies that possibility through a complex suppression of the sexual body.

As Mary Smith's interpretive involvement here suggests, the sexual discretion of the narrative—its erasure of sexuality and the erotic body—could be attributed to its narrator. Because Mary Smith lives in Drumble, making extended visits to Cranford, she is in a sense suspended between the codes of Cranford and the larger world, perfectly positioned both to satirize Cranford's repression and to duplicate it. Gaskell, however, determines the plot of the novel, which is predicated precisely on the recurrent death or disappearance of the novel's males in order to remove the threat of sexuality from the narrative. That this plot device is not simply invoked to create an Amazon utopia is evidenced by the fact that the narrative also excises sexualized women. Major Gordon and Miss Jessie Brown marry and leave Cranford, and Lady Glenmire essentially drops out of the narrative upon her marriage to Mr. Hoggins. If one of the points of Gaskell's novel is that the opposition of culture and nature, of genteel codes and the "facts of life," is unstable because of its artificiality, liable to collapse in the face of the sexual, the narrative as a whole still attempts to maintain the opposition.

Writing at midcentury, Gaskell thus presents a central paradox of the status of the sexual in Victorian literature and culture. If Gaskell is aware of the inevitable failure of any attempt to delimit the "cultural" from the "natural," if she is conscious of the artificiality of sexual repression, she nonetheless unconsciously participates in such repression. Unlike the Cranford ladies, this is not because Gaskell fears nature's chaotic disruptions of ordered social codes. Rather, Gaskell's sexual reticence derives from her concern to maintain other differences crucial to the social structure. Despite Gaskell's satire on Cranford's class assumptions, one of these differences is the taxonomy of the class system, as another incident involving Martha suggests. Preparing for a visit from her cousin, the major, and his wife, a flustered Matty attempts to explain the etiquette of serving to the recently hired Martha:

> "And mind you go first to the ladies," put in Miss Matilda. "Always go to the ladies before gentlemen, when you are waiting."
> "I'll do as you tell me, ma'am," said Martha; "but I like lads best." (68)

Matty feels "very uncomfortable and shocked," as once again the passage indirectly confronts her genteel codes with the existence of the sexual. The introduction of Martha's perspective here goes even further, however, suggesting the existence of different class sexualities, of a working-class culture in which sexual interest is both clearly felt and freely acknowledged. Thus the reader realizes that if Cranford is a utopia for ladies above a certain social level because of the absence of men, it must also be a utopia for women below a certain social level precisely because handsome young men "abound in the lower classes."

As such, genteel repression can be seen as overdetermined. Not only does repression conceal the sexual in order to deny biological universality, but sexual repression itself serves as a class marker, a means of ideologically distinguishing the social classes. As Nancy Armstrong has demonstrated, during the 1830s middle-class anxiety over political disorder, the threat of working-class rebellion, was translated into a notion of the sexual disorder of the lower classes: of their promiscuity and lack of sexual self-restraint. Transposed into sexual terms, Armstrong notes, class anxiety was provided with a symbolic solution, namely, the presentation in fiction of hierarchical domestic spaces where sexual and social order is created under a woman's supervision (1987, 169–86). As such, the domestic ideal also contains a class ideal of the bourgeois woman, whose own sexual desire is self-regulated and who domesticates working-class desire from above through external controls. This is precisely the nature of the households within *Cranford,* given the Cranford ladies' concern to regulate the romantic lives of their maids, but the principle can be seen to extend further—into the "domestic space," supervised by both male and female writers, of the Victorian novel itself. The point is not simply that the bourgeois discretion of Victorian fiction serves the parallel function of restraining the working-class sexuality it hints at, that Martha's sexual perspective is "regulated" through Gaskell's depiction of it. Finally, the novelist's own sexual discretion stands as evidence of the difference of the social classes. As a middle class attitude, the genteel repression of both characters and novelist creates precisely the premise (the difference of the classes) on which it is ostensibly based. Thus, although Gaskell satirizes Cranford's notion of the ontological differences between the classes as naive, the discretion of her own narrative implicitly insists on class difference. Based on a rewriting of class as differing sexual attitudes, genteel repression enacts, as an "internal" moral difference, precisely the fantasy of class difference as ontological, as a difference in kind, that Gaskell overtly mocks. In a sense, then, genteel repression insists on the reality of the phenomenon that it produces.[3]

If Gaskell thus demonstrates the sophistication of Victorian sexual ideology, the sexual nonetheless produces a logical contradiction, a conceptual double bind, at the core of the novel, turning Gaskell's satire back on itself. The problem is that the sexual must be represented (indeed Gaskell's satire insists on it) at the same time that, as the discretion of the novel reveals, to do so would be to erase a distinguishing mark of class difference. Although one of the themes of the book is the inescapability of biology, its continual tendency to shatter cultural codes, Gaskell herself adheres to the parallel codes of novelistic discretion. As it happens, Gaskell's difficulties are both complicated and resolved by another issue central to the novel: gender difference. Calling contemporary definitions of gender into question, Gaskell not only suggests some of the additional dangers of sexuality, she also confronts and resolves the problems of representing the sexual.

GENDER TROUBLE

In this village of the Amazons, gender begins to seem as slippery as the sex of the beggar who appears at Miss Pole's door during the Panic. Initially described as a woman with masculine features, she undergoes a metamorphosis with each retelling of the story until she becomes a man dressed in women's clothes with "a beard on her chin, and a manly voice and a stride" (145). Miss Pole's imaginative transformation of the beggar's gender is entirely appropriate to a village in which the current rector is as nervous about marriage as "any girl of eighteen" and attends the magic show surrounded by a group of National School boys as if he were a "queen-bee." What the rector lacks in conventional masculine behavior is more than compensated for, however, by Deborah Jenkyns. The epitome of the "strong-minded woman," Deborah is noted for the "dragoon-like" forcefulness of her acts of charity and for her attire: she wears a cravat and a little bonnet that is "half-helmet, half jockey cap" (57). Deborah's masculine attributes can be explained by her status as the leader of Cranford's Amazons, but the full implications of her sartorial and behavioral choices become clear only in relation to the transvestism of another member of the Jenkyns family, Deborah's brother Peter.

As Miss Matty explains to Mary Smith, Peter was notorious in his youth for his pranks and hoaxes, although his jokes do seem to fall into a predictable pattern. He takes in his father, for example, by dressing up as a lady who wishes to meet the Reverend Jenkyns because she admires the sermon he has published. As Matty notes, the joke backfires when the Reverend Jenkyns sets Peter to work copying out "all his Napoleon Buonaparte sermons for her—him, I mean—no, her, for Peter was a lady then" (94). Comic as it is, Matty's confusion hints at part of the reason for the instability of gender in *Cranford*. If the women of Cranford repress awareness of the body, this repression poses obvious problems for the (cultural) definition of gender. Cranford's notion of gender difference is in fact based implicitly on physical characteristics, as Miss

Pole's reference to the beggar's beard suggests, but this basis must remain largely unexpressed. In deference to the code of gentility, anatomical differences between the sexes are repressed and displaced onto clothing, which not only conceals the body but, because clothing itself is (conventionally) gendered, reinscribes the hidden anatomical differences on the surface. The result is that, in a sense, one's gender is determined by one's clothing. At least for Miss Matty, if Peter was dressed as a lady, then Peter *was* a lady.

Gaskell is not as naive as Matty, but Peter's second prank reveals that Gaskell herself is unwilling to resort to the anatomical as a means of grounding gender difference. Vexed with Deborah, Peter decides to take revenge, as Matty explains: "Well! he went to her room, it seems, and dressed himself in her old gown, and shawl, and bonnet; just the things she used to wear in Cranford, and was known by everywhere; and he made the pillow into a little—you are sure you locked the door, my dear, for I should not like anyone to hear—into—into—a little baby, with white long clothes. . . . And he went and walked up and down in the Filbert walk—just half hidden by the rails, and half seen; and he cuddled his pillow, just like a baby; and talked to it all the nonsense people do" (95). Precisely at this point, the Reverend Jenkyns returns home to find a crowd of people looking through his garden rails. Convinced at first that they are admiring his new rhododendron, he soon realizes that they are contemplating a less natural beauty, and "swift as light, he was in at the garden door, and down the Filbert walk, and seized hold of poor Peter, and tore his clothes off his back—bonnet, shawl, gown, and all—and threw the pillow among the people over the railings: and then he was very, very angry indeed; and before all the people he lifted up his cane, and flogged Peter!" (96).

Because Peter's assumption of his sister's identity has been based on dressing in her clothes, his father's act of revelation must logically be based on removing those clothes. What is striking here, however, is that readers are not told, as they would be in a modern novel, what lies under the clothes—namely, Peter's own body. This omission is of particular importance because Peter's cross-dressing confirms Marjorie Garber's assertion that transvestism, by denaturalizing the sartorial signs of gender, ultimately implies the instability of gender categories themselves (1992, 147). As such, the reverend's response must be to assert the "reality" of gender difference, but Gaskell herself is unwilling to base this reality on the body. Her own sense of decorum diverts the reader's gaze from Peter's gendered body to the father's activity. Even if we do not dwell on the symbolic resonances of the cane, the reverend's behavior here insists on the immutability of gender difference by implicitly appealing to gendered codes of behavior, conventional gender roles. Acting out the role of the father, whose word is law and whose function is to distinguish and separate, the Reverend Jenkyns responds to the situation with the aggression and violence traditionally associated with masculine behavior. Both the aim of his activity (to distinguish Peter and Deborah, male and female) and its violent mode imply that if gender difference cannot be based on the repressed body or the unstable semiotics of clothing, then it must be grounded behaviorally, on traditional gender roles and codes of action.

The incident does not end with the flogging of Peter, however, and its sequel undermines the father's attempt to establish the "reality" of gender. Humiliated, Peter comes into the storeroom where Matty and her mother are making cowslip wine, and "looking like a man, not like a boy," he bids his mother farewell. Peter runs off to join the navy, eventually losing touch with his family, and as Matty says, "That boy's trick . . . broke my mother's heart, and changed my father for life" (96). Reverend Jenkyns becomes "very gentle"; Mrs. Jenkyns, in fact, dies of grief. The episode thus represents a curious dislocation of the gendered positions of the Victorian family structure that Freud would soon institutionalize as the Oedipal crisis. Peter becomes a man not by manifesting a desire to *have* the mother but, on the deepest level, by attempting to *be* her, and the incident leads not to the symbolic death of the father or the recognition of the mother's castration but to the literal death of the mother and the symbolic castration of the father. Chastened, the Reverend Jenkyns is now "so humble." Although he sometimes speaks "in his old way—laying down the law," he "comes round" in a minute or two, asking "in a low voice" if he has said anything to hurt anyone (101). Abdicating masculine power and the role of the father as law, the reverend, from a Victorian perspective, has been "feminized," and the paternal role is undertaken by Deborah, who forgoes matrimony to take care of (and introject the masculine qualities of) her father. If this curious episode "makes a man" out of Peter, it also makes a woman out of his father and a man out of his sister.

Such crossings of the line of traditional gender roles confirm Shoshana Felman's assertion that these roles are themselves a set of costumes, "travesties" of "real" sexual difference that can be assumed or rejected at will (1981, 28–29). It becomes clear that gender cannot be based on behavioral codes. Because Gaskell does not resort to the body, gender, it is suggested, can be only a cultural fiction. Although this notion is appropriate for a work devoted to a village of Amazons, Gaskell does not seem entirely comfortable with the idea. One realizes that the gender instability of the Jenkyns family leads not only to behavioral chaos but also to celibacy and spinsterhood, an end to reproduction that is aptly symbolized by the mother's death. Having hinted at the fictionality of gender, Gaskell seems afraid of the implications of this assertion and anxious to establish the validity of nineteenth-century gender distinctions.

This anxiety is subtly apparent in Gaskell's use of adjectives. When Captain Brown is introduced into the narrative, he is characterized by his "masculine common sense" and "manly frankness," and he deals with his daughter's illness with "manly pious resignation." Captain Brown is not the only male character marked by such adjectives. The carter who announces Brown's death has a "manly" face, and the youthful letters of the Reverend Jenkyns to his future wife evince the "warmth of a manly heart." By the time, however, that Mary Smith announces that the Reverend Jenkyns dealt with Peter's expulsion from Shrewsbury in a "manly way" by tutoring the boy himself, it becomes apparent that the use of terms such as *masculine* or *manly* serves less to denote a set of clearly defined gender characteristics than to empty the terms of any real meaning whatsoever. *Manly* comes finally not to represent a transcendental masculine essence but to suggest Gaskell's nervous insistence that such an essence must exist.[4] If Gaskell's use of adjectives serves less to denote "real" gender differences than to demonstrate her desire to distinguish the genders, the text is nonetheless finally grounded on a set of differences between the sexes. Although Peter's prank serves to problematize the idea of gender, it also suggests a basis for gender distinctions in the differing relations of men and women to the central figure of the scene: the baby.

In *Cranford,* the concept of woman's "nature" is most clearly illustrated in the story of Signora Brown, which presents an ideal of motherhood that defines a conception of the feminine. Having accompanied her husband to India, the Signora gives birth to six children, only to lose them all to the climate. When the seventh is born, she decides to walk to Calcutta to book passage back to England in order to save her child's life. Preparing to set off on her journey, the Signora pays a visit to an officer's wife to ask if she may have a picture, "done by a Catholic foreigner," of the Virgin and the infant Jesus: "She had him on her arm, and her form was softly curled round him and their cheeks touched" (160). Having lost her own children, the officer's wife gives the print to the Signora. The painting is an apt illustration of the idea of motherhood in the novel. As Julia Kristeva has pointed out, the emblem of the Virgin Mary and the baby Jesus represents a conception of motherhood as paradoxical: as a physically distinct being, the child is separate from and alien to the mother, yet this other has come, quite literally, from the self. The relation of mother and child thus blurs the distinction of self and other (Kristeva 1986, 117). This principle is suggested in the print not only by the touching of cheeks, the linking of the physically distinct bodies of mother and child, but also by the circular shape of the painting. Curled around each other, the Virgin and the "little Saviour" represent the relations of mother and child as a circle, an endless movement from self to other and back again.

Here Gaskell implicitly invokes women's reproductive capacity as the basis of woman's "nature." In so doing, she illustrates a common Victorian tendency. The idea of motherhood or of an innate "maternal instinct" grounded contemporary definitions of "woman," providing a basis for the idea that women are inherently self-sacrificing and that women's social relations involve, in consequence, the continual erasure of rigid distinctions between self and other (Poovey 1988, 6; Russett 1989, 43).[5] Thus the portrait episode centers on a process of identification of all mothers and all children, and the Signora's request and the lady's gift are based on a mutual awareness of their identity with each other and with the subject of the painting. Implicitly, the Signora *is* the officer's wife *is* the Virgin Mary. As such, the concept of "foreignness" itself disappears: the Protestant Signora is not troubled by the provenance of the painting as a Catholic icon, and she in fact stops to pray in a "native temple" because the place "where others had prayed before to their God" must be of itself "sacred" (161). Differing religions and deities blur into one. Similarly, private property, the material extension of a belief in the distinction of self and other, ceases to exist: the portrait freely changes hands. Moreover, the refusal to distinguish self and other means that even communication involves an identification with the other, a pre-linguistic "correspondence of bodies" (Kristeva 1986, 114). As the Signora says, the language barrier posed no problems during her travels through India: "The natives were very kind. We could not understand one another; but they saw my baby on my breast, and they came out to me, and brought me rice and milk, and some-times flowers" (161). Symbolized here by the circulation of food from the natives to the mother and from mother to child, interac-tion is based on an understanding deeper than words whose model is, finally, the prenatal, umbilical connection of mother and child.

The Signora's story thus begins to suggest a foundation for gender difference, adumbrating an idea of the feminine based on and epitomized in motherhood. As such, it seems hardly acciden-tal that the Signora's narrative is interpolated in the middle of a discussion about her husband and his twin brother Thomas, for, as twins, the brothers implicitly demonstrate an alternate view of the relations of self and other that is linked to a male fantasy of repro-duction. Like mother and child, twins problematize the notions of sameness and difference but in another fashion. If patriarchy is homosocial, based on relations between men, with women serv-ing merely as a means of mediation between males (Irigaray 1985, 192–93), at its most extreme, this doctrine finds expression in the masculine ideal of the son as the exact duplicate of the father, the product of a phantasmic biology in which the woman makes no genetic contribution to the child but serves merely as a conduit through which the father creates the son. Unlike the mother's relation to her child, the father's wish to see himself duplicated in the son is not a desire for connection with an other but rather the wish for replication of the self in a form distinct from the self. The male ideal, then, is the copy, which implies not only the primacy of the original (the father) over the duplicate (the son) but a linear movement: the physical distinctness of the son ensures the father a certain immortality. In contrast to the feminine model of repro-duction—in which the blurred identities of mother and child, of all mothers and all children, make the primacy of the self impossible and subvert linearity in a continual circular identification—the masculine ideal is grounded on the distinction of self and other, on the principle of distinction itself. In the male twin, this principle is merely displaced laterally. Here it is Sam's brother Thomas whose likeness to Sam allows him to carry on "Signor Brunoni's" magic show after Sam is injured, Sam being presented as the authentic original of Thomas's inferior copy. In fact, the stress here is on difference rather than similarity. Although the Signora says that the likeness between the brothers has allowed them to pull off any number of magic tricks, she cannot conceive "how people can mistake Thomas for the real Signor" (158).

Gender difference in *Cranford* can thus be seen to rest on two ideas of reproduction that imply differing, gendered conceptions of the relation of self and other.[6] In one sense, however, Gaskell's suggestion of the "real" basis of gender difference seems to raise more questions than it answers. It seems paradoxical, for example, that the difference between men and women should be illustrated by differing conceptions of reproduction, when the Cranford ladies are so concerned to repress the sexual and biological. While Miss Matty's intense desire for a child may illustrate the "essential" femininity of her nature, serving as a sign of her selflessness, how is the reader to reconcile this desire with her difficulties in merely saying the word *baby*? Similarly, if Gaskell herself manifests a genteel refusal to resort to the facts of the body to determine gender, how can she present male and female ideals of reproduction as the key to understanding the sexes? Her own construction of gender difference seems to rely on a sexuality and biology that Gaskell herself is reluctant to express. As we shall see, however, Gaskell's definition of the genders in fact allows her both to clarify and to neutralize the threatening aspects of sexuality and sexual desire. More significantly, it also provides a solution to the problems of representing the sexual.

FEMALE TROUBLE

Peter's prank recalls the dangers posed by sexuality to Cranford's social order. It is worth noting that Peter's conscious intention here is not to call traditional gender distinctions into question or even to enact woman's relation to the child or the other. Vexed with Deborah because she finds him "ungenteel," Peter aims to "plague her," and his assertion that he is not being malicious but only trying to "make something to talk about in town" seems disingenuous. In fact, the incident is an attempt to impute to Deborah the essence of the "ungenteel," the scandal of sexuality, for the illegitimate child is the ultimate symbol of the threat posed by biology to the rules and codes, the "legitimacy," of culture. In essence, this imaginary baby represents the irrelevance of cultural institutions such as marriage to the facts of procreation.

Gaskell's definition of the genders transforms, however, the symbolic implications of the baby, purging reproduction of its sexual implications. For one thing, the novel's view of reproduction is finally an ideal of a biology without sexuality: sexual facts are excluded from the discussion. Thus, the Signora's story begins *after* her child is born, and the male ideal of reproduction is displaced onto the relation of brothers rather than focusing on the father's (pro)creation of the son. Appropriately, the central image of the mother in the novel is the Virgin Mary, that icon of conception "untainted by man or sex" (Kristeva 1986, 114), and just as Peter is able to create a "baby" without recourse to biology, so Miss Matty is finally provided with the child she has always wanted as if by divine intervention. Completely unaware of Martha's pregnancy, Matty is presented with a child to care for without ever having to confront the sexuality excluded from Cranford's code of gentility.

But the image of the "virginal maternal" does not simply serve to repress awareness of sexuality. Gaskell's delineation of gender difference suggests an even deeper reason for the Cranford ladies' fear of sexuality than the threat it poses to attempts to distinguish culture and nature or to erect a class taxonomy. Given woman's imperfect distinction of self and other, the fusion of two into one in the sexual relation is threatening because it implies the disappearance of the woman. As Mary Poovey has pointed out, the juridical relation of the genders in the Victorian period was governed by the common-law notion of "coverture," the doctrine that the wife is subsumed legally in her husband (1988, 51–52). *Cranford* can thus be seen as a depiction of the anxiety produced in women by the workings of this doctrine in the sexual sphere. Given belief in woman's fluid relation to others and male emphasis on the primacy of the self, sexuality raises the possibility that the woman will be completely submerged in the man's identity. The point is summarized metaphorically on the first page of the novel. Discussing the self-sufficiency of the Cranford ladies, Mary Smith stresses their desire to do "good offices" for each other and to obtain an intimate knowledge of each other's affairs. They are also "sufficient," however, for "keeping the trim gardens full of choice flowers without a weed to speck them; for frightening away little boys who look wistfully at the said flowers through the railings; for rushing out at the geese that occasionally venture into the gardens if the gates are left open" (39). The passage suggests a central principle of Cranford life: the women's desire to distinguish an inviolable enclave. The novel, in fact, is dominated by a fear of male invasion of a feminine space, whether the space is conceived as the town of Cranford itself or, in the case of the Panic, the homes of the Cranford ladies. Here that space, implying both the feminine body and the self, is the garden, and the Cranford ladies' thwarting of attempts to invade this territory subtly suggests their resistance to the linked threats of literal, corporeal penetration and of psychological "colonization," the annexation of the psychic "space" of the self by the male.[7] Woman's sense of her fluid relation to the other in *Cranford* is thus directed toward nonsexual contacts with other women, an evasion of the danger of the disappearance of the self posed by sexuality and by men. It seems hardly accidental then that the babies who appear in the novel, those symbols of the blurring of self and other, are all female, from little Phoebe Brown to Martha's daughter Matilda.

Sexuality, finally, is threatening to the world of Cranford not only because of its power to disrupt cultural organization but also because, for the woman, it erases another difference: the distinction of self and other. The anxiety would seem to be shared—in a more sophisticated fashion—by Gaskell herself. If the Cranford ladies' sexual anxiety is presented comically and if Gaskell freely acknowledges, as the Cranford ladies do not, that women cannot really live without men, Gaskell's solution to this problem nonetheless suggests her own, presumably unconscious, anxiety about the loss of feminine identity. Despite their disclaimers, the Cranford ladies' ties to other women are not sufficient to meet their needs for intimacy, as Matty's grief over Holbrook's death suggests. Peter's return provides a solution to the problem, however. Initially, the general expectation that Peter will marry Mrs. Jamieson would seem to raise precisely the male threat of the submersion of the woman in marriage that Cranford fears. As it turns out, however, Peter's attentions to Mrs. Jamieson are intended merely to reconcile her to the Hogginses because the quarrel disturbs Miss Matty, and the novel ends, not in Peter's literal marriage to Mrs. Jamieson, but in his figurative marriage to Matty. Matty and Peter thus represent the nonsexual union of male and female without the complete dissolution of the woman's identity, as Peter's concern with Matty's peace of mind implies. Resolving the pain of loneliness, this "family romance," located precisely in a fantasy of the family as a presexual, pre-Oedipal realm, allows the union of male and female, self and other without the dangerous implications of sexuality. Like the image of the virginal maternal, this fantasy of the "virginal matrimonial" allows Gaskell to present an "innocent biology" (sibling consanguinity) purged of the sexual and thus to resolve an ideological conflict, allowing her to posit intimate relations between the genders that do not provoke the loss of feminine identity implicit in sexual relations.

REPRESENTING THE SEXUAL

We can thus see too how Gaskell resolves the implicit difficulties of representing the sexual. Although the content of the novel continually insists that Cranford's attempts to ignore the biological and the sexual are doomed to failure, Gaskell herself is reluctant to directly articulate sexuality or the "facts" of the body. In effect, paradoxically, the sexual both must be and cannot be spoken. By displacing the problem onto the issue of gender difference, an issue that is itself raised by her refusal to represent the body, Gaskell is able not only to articulate and resolve her unconscious anxieties about gender relations but also, finally, to solve the problem of novelistic representation of the sexual.

I have already suggested the outlines of this solution in Gaskell's use of the family at the novel's end. Because family relations are conceived along two axes, as a set of social roles and a set of biological relations, Gaskell is simultaneously able to imply and to mystify the biological basis of the family by conflating it with the cultural idea of the family. Presented primarily as a social unit in the novel, the family nonetheless retains its biological and sexual associations, so that such associations are both invoked and occluded. A clearer version of the same principle obtains in Gaskell's presentation of gender. As Mary Poovey has demonstrated, and as *Cranford* itself suggests, Victorian definitions of woman derive not simply from woman's reproductive function but from *readings* of the "meaning" of her reproductive physiology (1988, 24–50). Thus the idea of a "maternal instinct" that defines woman as selfless is implicitly based on a notion of the female body that is lost in its translation into a feminine psychological "essence."[8] The etiology of such representations, their abstraction from a (suppressed) sexual body, allows Gaskell to exploit this process by duplicating it in her text. Thus "reproduction" and "gender" are suspended between their original biological and sexual associations and their definition in the novel in terms of their "cultural" implications: what they suggest for social relations. As such, Gaskell is able to redirect our attention from the sexual aspects of both gender and reproduction and focus it on their psychological and social effects. This strategy allows Gaskell to seem to be presenting the sexual and the biological without actually doing so. In a sense, the sexual both is and is not represented.

Gaskell thus solves the problem of representing the sexual precisely by invoking, on the textual level, the instability of the culture/nature distinction that so troubles the women of Cranford in the content of the novel. Playing on the simultaneous status of such ideas as "reproduction" or "gender" or "the family" as "natural" (biological and sexual "facts") and as "cultural" (social or psychological relations), Gaskell manipulates the instability of the distinction of culture and nature in order not only to represent the sexual but also to resolve the double bind produced by the need both to speak and to conceal sex and sexuality. If speaking the sexual would erase the erotic discretion that marks the difference between the bourgeoisie and the working class and if not speaking the sexual problematizes gender difference by erasing the body on which it is ostensibly based, Gaskell's solution—invoking without actually representing the sexual—resolves the contradiction and implicitly allows her to maintain the viability of class and gender differences.[9]

By way of conclusion, we can turn to the significance of the novel's ending. If both Cranford and much of *Cranford* are predicated on the expulsion of men and sexualized women, the principle operating at the novel's end is not exclusion but inclusion. Not only do men reenter Cranford, but the final festivities at the Assembly Room include the entire community and involve the reappearance of all the characters who have left Cranford, from Miss Jessie Brown to Signor Brunoni. "No one," says Mary Smith, "was forgotten." In fact, even the male characters who have died return in memory. The point is not simply that men or the vulgar facts are incorporated into Cranford society, transforming it. If Peter can entrance the Cranford ladies by sitting cross-legged on the floor, although Mr. Hoggins was previously condemned merely for crossing his legs, this does not mean that Cranford's genteel culture has evaporated. Instead, Gaskell is illustrating the power of cultural fictions, in this case the Cranford ladies' tendency to see Peter's posture as an elegant imitation of Mohammed rather than to note its resemblance to Simon Jones the tailor. Having begun by asserting the inescapability of biology, Gaskell ends by implying the power of culture, the mind's tendency to transform the "natural," to shape and structure it. Just as the Cranford ladies learn to mediate between the "facts" of biology and the "fictions" of culture, Gaskell herself resolves the difficulties of representing the sexual through a similar mediation, its inclusion in the novel through a manipulation of cultural ideology. If Jane Austen, like the Cranford ladies, argues for the necessary repression of sexuality and sexual desire, Gaskell's strategy for the possibility of sexual representation is not to reject "nature" but to embrace the fictions of culture.

Charles Dickens's *Bleak House,* to which the next chapter is devoted, can stand as something of a companion piece to *Cranford* in its investigation of the problems posed by the representation of sex and sexuality at midcentury. If Gaskell, like Austen, is primarily concerned with the potentially disruptive effects of the sexual on the social order, Dickens elaborates an additional danger of the sexual: Victorian perceptions of its potential to destabilize the self, to problematize the idea of identity. For the writer, this problem is compounded by the codes of novelistic discretion. Just as Gaskell struggles to define "gender" without recourse to the body, so Dickens, equally concerned to erase the physicality of his characters in order to evade the erotic, must articulate a basis for identity without invoking the physical body upon which the notion of identity is so often founded. Like Gaskell's reworking of cultural fictions, Dickens solves these difficulties by manipulating the fictionality of fiction itself. As we shall see, the problems of representing the sexual, the problems of sexuality itself, are redeemed in *Bleak House* by the sexuality of representation.

CHAPTER 4

The Text as Body: The Mystery of Sexuality in *Bleak House*

Like most mystery novels, *Bleak House* is a whodunit based on the discovery of a body and a question of identity, the identity of the killer. The novel's mysteries, however, are not confined to the murder of Tulkinghorn or solved by the arrest of Hortense. The bodies of Nemo, Lady Dedlock, and Krook raise their own questions—about causes of death and about the identity of the deceased. The central mystery of *Bleak House* suggests that the novel is also a whodunit of another sort. The question of Esther's origin, of the creation rather than the destruction of a body, generates numerous attempts by both characters and reader to determine the identity of Esther's parents and, hence, Esther's own identity. Just as the true mystery in detective novels is ultimately not the circumstances of a murder but the enigma of death itself, the core of *Bleak House* is the discovery not of *a* body but of *the* body—the mystery of sexuality that haunts Victorian culture and Victorian fiction. As we shall see, Dickens's characters struggle with the riddles of the biological and their relation to questions of identity, and Dickens himself encounters a parallel difficulty: the problem of representing and yet controlling the mysteries of the body. The problem, finally, of the "identity" of the text itself.

THE ENIGMAS OF DEATH AND BIRTH

In order to understand the place of the biological in *Bleak House,* we must begin with our end—with death. For both major and minor characters, the novel is a singularly unhealthy work in which

84

to appear. The deaths of Tulkinghorn, Coavinses, Richard, Jo, Krook, Lady Dedlock, Jenny's unnamed child, Gridley, Miss Barbary, and Nemo combine to produce a mortality rate for the characters of roughly 15 percent.[1] Like the novel's focus on illness and disease, this attention to death helps to stress the plight of the poor and the abuses of the Court of Chancery. Death in *Bleak House,* however, serves less to symbolize social evils than to undermine social satire itself. Dickens's criticism of Chancery is based, in part, on its disjunction from the cycle of human time, so that the "legion of bills in the suit" are transformed into "mere bills of mortality" long before *Jarndyce vs. Jarndyce* is resolved (Dickens [1852-53] 1964, 20). The novel's presentation of death, however, ultimately suggests that this disjunction of the judicial system and the demands of the body is less the product of bureaucratic lethargy than a result of the radical otherness of biology, which is alien not only to social institutions but to the explanatory powers of human reason. Death, the novel repeatedly insists, is "the last great secret" (584) in a novel obsessed with secrets, and like Jo, none of us "can exactly say" what happens after death.[2] Incomprehensible, death itself becomes a sign of the enigmatic in the novel. Thus Esther sees the Thames at night as fearful because it is "so death-like and mysterious" (774), and Tulkinghorn's impenetrability is repeatedly troped as being like that of death; he contains more secrets, we are told, than a mausoleum (26).

The genesis of the individual, where he or she "comes from," is perhaps even more mysterious than the end of the biological cycle. As Garrett Stewart has demonstrated, death in literature is the moment where content gives way to form, where the "imponderables of negation and vacancy" are "postponed" by the language of the text (1984, 3-7). The death scene in Dickens, Stewart argues, thus strains against the limitations of human knowledge, attempting to articulate the unknowable (1978, 443-87). In *Bleak House,* however, Dickens continually refuses to attempt a similar articulation of the parallel mystery of birth. To begin with, by centering the novel on the secret of Esther's conception, Dickens reinscribes the enigma of human origin in a more comforting form. If we cannot know exactly where we came from, the novel suggests, we can at least learn *who* we came from, and the ineffability of the biological thus becomes susceptible to detection, to reason.

What is striking about the novel, however, is that although we do eventually discover the identity of Esther's parents, this is virtually all that we learn. Unlike the mysterious deaths in the narrative, which are resolved by detectives and inquests, their circumstances fully elucidated, the whys and wherefores of sex are never truly clarified. Esther's birth is mysterious because of the suppression by both characters and narrator of Lady Dedlock's sexuality, but all that is ever revealed is that this sexuality exists. The reader is never made privy to the circumstances leading to Esther's conception. Such information is presumably contained in the letter that Lady Dedlock gives to Esther, but having burned the letter, the fire destroying "even its ashes," Esther explains only how her mother came to think her child was dead. Equally crucial questions go unanswered, at least for the reader: how Captain Hawdon and Lady Dedlock met, the circumstances of their lapse into illicit sexuality, why they failed to marry. Although Esther says that "what more the letter told me needs not to be repeated here. It has its own times and places in my story" (520), such times and places never come, and the reader must content himself with Tulkinghorn's coded narrative at Chesney Wold, which adds only the information that the "lady" was engaged to "the young rake" (579).

If the sexuality of Esther's mother is left unexamined, the sexuality of her father is even further mystified, evident only in Tulkinghorn's fleeting, stereotypical characterization of him as an aristocratic roué. Given this absence of any analysis of the psychology of sexual desire, it is hardly surprising that the novel circles around a sexual scene that is itself strikingly absent. Giving birth not only to Esther but to much of the narrative, this primal scene cannot itself be narrated.[3] Such silence is continually reproduced in the novel, which consistently suppresses any reference to sexuality or sexual desire. In fact, even love is frequently shrouded in secrecy in *Bleak House:* in Richard and Ada's initial ignorance of their mutual feelings or in their clandestine marriage or even in Caddy Jellyby and Prince Turveydrop's secret engagement. Most striking, however, is Esther's oft-noted narrative coyness in relation to Woodcourt, in which her feelings for Allan are evident for much of the novel precisely through absence, through her reluctance to narrate her encounters with him, and in her continual disclaimers that these narrative lapses mean anything at all. Coming most often at the end of chapters, Esther's romantic suppressions stand both literally and figuratively on the verge of silence, the rule rather than the exception to the novel's presentation of the romantic and the sexual.

IDENTITY CRISES

If Dickens attempts to articulate the mysteries of death, why does *Bleak House* demonstrate this complex retreat from those other "facts" of biology—sex and sexuality? The difficulty of speaking the sexual in *Bleak House,* the threat it poses, would seem at first to revolve around questions of legitimacy. The dangerous liaison of Lady Dedlock and Captain Hawdon and the illegitimate birth resulting from it clearly illustrate Victorian perceptions of the tendency of biological drives to violate the rules of culture, whether these rules are the cultural distinctions of licit and illicit sexual activity that regulate sexual relations or the related distinction of legitimate and illegitimate birth derived from them. Stress on the licit and illicit is evident not only in Miss Barbary's assertion to Esther that "your mother . . . is your disgrace, and you were hers" (33) but in the related assumption, articulated by Tulking-horn and shared by Lady Dedlock herself, that Lady Dedlock is so "tainted" that Rosa's mere association with her will ruin the girl's chances for a decent marriage. Based on religious principles, as Miss Barbary's adherence to it suggests, the ideal of female purity violated by Lady Dedlock transcends its moral implications in the course of the novel.[4] The problems posed by Lady Dedlock's "fall" are ultimately less religious or spiritual (questions about sin and salvation) than sociological (questions about the integration of individuals into the social structure). The danger of Lady Dedlock's breaking of cultural sexual codes is that it leads to social disorientation—to the vexing question of how the illegitimate child, born outside the rules of culture, can find a place within society, and to Lady Dedlock's own loss of her social "place," a loss symbolically affirmed in her assumption of the clothes, and marginal social status, of Jenny and literally enacted in her flight from London and eventual death. If Rosa can be "tainted" by Lady Dedlock, it is not because she would be magically contaminated by vice but because, equally magically, she would be touched by the possibility of social dis-integration, by an inability to marry.

Unlike Austen and Gaskell, however, Dickens does not finally seem particularly troubled by the antitaxonomic properties of sexual desire, by its ability to violate cultural structures.[5] If Lady Dedlock is expelled from society, Esther, in contrast, has little difficulty finding a place in it. Provided by Jarndyce with a role as mistress of Bleak House, Esther is also presented with a series of marriage proposals, both the sign of social acceptability and the offer of further integration into the social structure. Moreover, Dickens is particularly concerned to address the question of illegitimacy, so that Mrs. Woodcourt's implicit objection to Esther's birth vanishes in her recognition of Esther's "true legitimacy" (860), a rewriting of the notion based on character rather than on the conformity of Esther's birth to social codes. If Dickens indeed does not stress the threat that the sexual poses to the social structure, why is sexuality so rigorously suppressed in the narrative? The answer is suggested by the shift of the concept of legitimacy from juridical to psychological terms. The danger posed by sexuality in *Bleak House* is less a question of external cultural structures than one of internal psychic organization. The problem with sexuality is not that it shatters the social order but that it unsettles the self.

If sexuality, the impulses of the body, is dangerous in *Bleak House,* this is because sexual activity produces a profound dislocation of identity, as Dickens suggests in his portraits of the mother, father, and child implicated in the sexual relation at the novel's core. The fragmentation of the self induced by sexuality can take a number of forms, but the most obvious is the internalization of the social disapprobation placed on the fallen woman or the illegitimate child. In a sense, this internalization is the implantation within the individual of the distinction between "natural" (or biological) and "cultural" (or social) relations that Gaskell manipulates in *Cranford,* the creation of a sense that the individual is split between a "social" identity and a "biological" identity, as the case of Lady Dedlock illustrates. Confronting Esther in the woods outside her country estate, an appropriately nonsocial space, Lady Dedlock notes to Esther that, "proud and disdainful" everywhere else, she will be humbled and ashamed here "in the only natural moments of her life" (517). She goes on to draw the contrast even more pointedly: "If you hear of Lady Dedlock, brilliant, prosperous, and flattered, think of your wretched mother, conscience-stricken, underneath that mask" (519-20). If Lady Dedlock is split between her identity as a "lady" and her identity as Esther's mother, between "social" and "biological" self-definitions, the revelation produces an equally profound crisis of identity in Esther.

In fact, the crisis has started earlier, during Esther's illness, and the novel draws a number of links between Esther's "disfigurement and [her] inheritance of shame" (617).[6] Even before smallpox alters Esther's appearance, producing a "new self," the illness shatters her identity. Febrile, Esther finds that the "divisions of time" in her life become confused: "At once a child, an elder girl, and the little woman I had been so happy as, I was not only oppressed by cares and difficulties adapted to each station, but by the great perplexity of trying to reconcile them" (495-96). Seen here not as the linear progression of a coherent entity through time but as a series of discrete temporal and ontological stages, the self as experienced during illness aptly forecasts Esther's difficulty in reconciling her birth with her current social station. Although the sexuality in question is her mother's and not her own, Esther internalizes her mother's guilt through a sort of contagion. Noting that she feels as if "the blame and the shame" are in her (521), Esther is stricken with a sense of a "natural" connection to her mother that is at odds with the social threat she poses to Lady Dedlock. Seeing her mother in a theater, Esther realizes that, biologically linked, they must be "wide asunder before the great company of all degrees" (597). This perception is ultimately manifested in Esther's "terror of myself," which replicates the internal separation of the biological and the social as an antagonistic division. Although her guilt is later dispelled because the sexuality involved is not her own, Esther's awareness of her "illegitimacy" nonetheless unsettles and divides her sense of identity.

If sexuality disrupts the self through the internalization of guilt, through the perception of a split between the "natural" and "cultural" selves, this fragmentation is consistently linked to death, the literal end of identity.[7] Thus Esther's perception is that it was "wrong and not intended that I should be then alive" (521) when she learns of her illegitimacy, just as Lady Dedlock insists that Esther must think of her mother as dead. The social "death" associated with illicit sexuality is metaphorically enacted when Guppy presents the results of his investigation into Esther's background to Lady Dedlock. As Guppy speaks, Lady Dedlock's face takes on a "dead colour," and when Guppy finally names Esther's father, Lady Dedlock becomes "for the moment dead," although the condition is transient, "like those long-preserved dead bodies sometimes opened up in tombs, which, struck by the air like lightning, vanish in a breath" (417).

As the latter phrase suggests, the passage also implies an additional link between sexuality and the "death" of the self, a metaphoric connection that is the inverse of the social mortality that can result from the revelation of sexual activity. The comparison between the uncovering of Lady Dedlock's secret and the opening of a tomb to disclose a "long-preserved dead body" implies the effects of sexual repression: the "death" of Lady Dedlock's "body," of her physicality, after the birth of her child. The psychic effects of such repression can be glossed by looking at another instance of the contagion of Lady Dedlock's sexuality—its effect on her sister, Miss Barbary. Indeed, it also allows us to interpret the otherwise puzzling analysis that Jarndyce gives to Esther of Miss Barbary's severed relationship with Boythorn. Since Esther's birth "injured" her "haughty spirit," Miss Barbary writes to Boythorn to end their relationship, informing him "that from the date of that letter she died to him," which, Jarndyce adds, "in literal truth she did" (611). Miss Barbary's "death" can be literal only if the effect of her sister's sexuality is to induce a psychic death, a repression of her own sexual impulses that causes Miss Barbary to embrace a sort of "death in life" that parallels and reproduces Lady Dedlock's own sexual repression. By the time the novel begins, Miss Barbary too is a "long-preserved dead body."

At first glance, Dickens would seem to be arguing against sexual repression and the harsh restraints of Miss Barbary's religion. The literal deaths of Lady Dedlock and Nemo, however, demonstrate that sexual indulgence is equally dangerous to the self. Ruskin's commentary on literal deaths in the novel in the first essay of "Fiction, Fair and Foul" ([1880] 1963) is suggestive in this context. Noting, somewhat inaccurately, that the novel contains nine deaths or "left for death's, in the drop scene," Ruskin continues with his own inquest into causes of death in *Bleak House*. Physical factors play a role, obviously, so that Tulkinghorn meets his fate through assassination and Jo dies of "starvation, with phthisis," but what is striking is Ruskin's attribution of Richard's death to "chagrin," Nemo's death to "sorrow," and Lady Dedlock's to "remorse." Conflating physical and psychological causes of death, Ruskin presents a rather curious epidemiology based on the assumption that intense emotional states can cause the literal disintegration of the individual. Dickens does not embrace this notion as transparently as Ruskin does. Nemo's death, after all, is attributed to an opium overdose. The morbid consequences of emotion, however, resonate throughout the novel. Thus Krook's death is in part symbolic, an enactment of the eventual implosion of the corrupt legal system for which he acts as a metaphor, but as Dickens repeatedly insisted, it is to be taken literally as well, as a genuine case of spontaneous combustion "engendered in the corrupted humours of the vicious body itself" (464). Also moved by strong emotions and desires, the corrupted humors of the body, Lady Dedlock and Nemo may not explode, but both of Esther's parents die, at least in part, from exhaustion, as if worn out by the passions that generated the narrative.

Passion would seem to lead, finally, not only to literal death but to a figurative one, the "exhaustion" of identity. If the sexual itself is never directly portrayed in *Bleak House,* the experience of sexuality is nonetheless re-presented in the novel through a loss of self that is seen as one of its aftereffects. Precisely because the reader is never enlightened on the actual trajectory of Captain Hawdon's life, it seems to be his liaison with Lady Dedlock that has turned him into "Nemo," a "no-one" who cannot be identified by the group surrounding his deathbed. The course of Nemo's life, however, can be inferred from its replication in Lady Dedlock's flight from London. Noting, in the letter she pens just before her death, that there is "nothing about me by which I can be recognized," Lady Dedlock's individual identity dissolves into a generic biological role. "Do not blame the mother for her share" (810), Lady Dedlock also writes, and the ambiguity of the phrase, which can refer both to Jenny and herself, stresses her potential biological interchangeability with any woman, an interchangeability confirmed by Esther's initial identification of Lady Dedlock as "the mother of the dead child." Despite Lady Dedlock's assertion that she will die of "terror and [her] conscience," death here seems finally less a punishment for "sin" than a literalization of the effects of passion, representing both the physical debilitation produced by intense feeling and the "wearing out" of identity, the expenditure of the self in the extreme emotions generated by sexuality. Just as Nemo's death establishes his pretensions to his name by making him "indeed no one," so Lady Dedlock's death confirms her loss of identity in her biological, reproductive role as "the mother" (153).[8]

SIGNS AND PERSONS: THE BODY AND IDENTITY

If the problem of sexuality in *Bleak House* is the threat it poses to identity, the solution to the problem, the means of evading such dangers, is not entirely clear, since both the practice of sexuality and its repression further the destruction of the self.[9] Nor is this simply a problem for the novel's characters. The difficulty of controlling the disruptive potential of sexuality without invoking the equally disastrous effects of repression is also apparent in a related, narrative arena: the novel's presentation of the body and its relation to identity, a representation epitomized by an incidental detail in Esther's story. Upon her first arrival in London, Esther is ushered into Kenge's office by Guppy, who calls her attention to a mirror in case she would like to "look at herself" after her journey. Esther's response is curious. She uses the looking glass to take "a peep at my bonnet . . . to see if it was neat" (45). As it happens, the deflection of Esther's attention from her face to her clothing enacts a familiar principle in the accounts of both narrators in *Bleak House,* in whose descriptions the bodies of the characters scarcely exist at all. To take an example more or less at random, the initial description of Sir Leicester Dedlock circles around the corporeal. Noting at first that Sir Leicester has an occasional "twist" of gout and that he walks stiffly, the narrator settles down to detail his appearance: "He is of a worthy presence, with his light-grey hair and whiskers, his fine shirt-frill, his pure-white waistcoat, and his blue coat with bright buttons always buttoned" (25). With a brief glance at the hair and whiskers, and reference to the more abstract notion of his "presence," the description proceeds to the clothing. The body, the site of the sexual, disappears.

In fact, the only parts of the body that appear in the narrative are the hands and face, the parts visible outside the clothes, as with Esther's first description of Ada as a "beautiful girl" with "such rich golden hair, such soft blue eyes, and such a bright,

92

innocent, trusting face" (45). Ada, here, is not merely reduced to a series of parts centered on the face, but these parts are less the particular characteristics of an individual than abstractions of a certain ideal of beauty. A similar process of generalization is evident even in characters who seem to be more fully described physically. Thus Mrs. Jellyby is a "pretty, very diminutive, plump woman of from forty to fifty, with handsome eyes, though they had a curious habit of seeming to look a long way off" (52). Just as Mrs. Jellyby's age is not specified but indicated as falling within a ten-year span, her body is abstracted, its characteristics detailed in terms ("pretty," "handsome," "plump") that are open to various constructions.

The exception to this generalization of Mrs. Jellyby's body is her eyes, her only specific physical attribute, which are primarily intended to suggest her devotion to "telescopic philanthropy." The body, or rather the face, is thus presented as an index of character, a means of discerning personality, as is even more evident in one of the novel's most detailed descriptions, the reader's introduction to Hortense. A Frenchwoman of thirty-two, Hortense is "a large-eyed brown woman with black hair who would be handsome but for a certain feline mouth and general uncomfortable tightness of face, rendering the jaws too eager and the skull too prominent. There is something indefinably keen and wan about her anatomy, and she has a watchful way of looking out of the corners of her eyes without turning her head which could be pleasantly dispensed with, especially when she is in an ill humour and near knives" (172). Hortense's character as a "she-wolf" is thus clear from her appearance, the face serving as a perfect representation of Hortense's nature. The stress on physical detail in such descriptions, however, is finally more apparent than real, for the characters are presented less as bodies than as embodiments, the physical merely serving to denote abstract qualities or psychological states. Thus Sir Leicester is ultimately an aristocratic "presence," intended primarily to represent the aristocracy in the work, and Mrs. Snagsby's nose, which is "like a sharp autumn evening, inclined to be frosty towards the end" (142), is adduced solely as an index of her shrewishness. The point is not simply that Dickens, like Austen and Gaskell, tends to ignore or generalize the body, but that the body here is less important than the personality traits it signals. By itself, the corporeal scarcely exists. In effect, the body in *Bleak House* becomes a sign whose materiality vanishes in its signifying function.[10]

In Dickens's novel, the suppression of the body that is common in Victorian fiction thus receives a particular inflection: not only does it restrict the presentation of biology in the narrative, but it also converts the body, the material locus of the sexual impulses that threaten identity, into a sign that insists on that identity. Given Dickens's focus on identity, however, *Bleak House* uncovers a problem with the erasure of the body in the Victorian novel that remains latent in *Pride and Prejudice* and *Cranford*. This difficulty becomes evident when we consider Gayatri Spivak's distinction between signs and people: "By phonocentric convention a sign means something other than itself whereas a person is self-proximate, even self-identical" (1986, 226). Thus if Dickens represses the body in narrative, this repression itself finally calls identity into question. Both in literature and in life, for example, the discovery of the corpse that initiates the murder narrative begins with an "identification": the recognition of the body of the victim as a specific "person" who exists prior to representation, prior to the reading of the body as the index of the individual's personality or to characterizations of his or her "nature." It is in this sense that the "person," the individual body, is tautological, self-identical. Once the body is "signed," its external physical features read as indications of "character," the body and the identity it represents become "ex-centric," a semiotic construct in which the individual is always "other" than himself or herself.

Literary characters are always already signs, verbal constructs, and it is one of the traditions of literature that the bodies of characters are themselves representational, texts in which personality and moral values can be read. Such conventions, however, depend on the illusion that the distinction between the body and the sign exists in literary works as well, that the "physical" bodies of the characters exist prior to any interpretation of them. This principle and its implications can be illustrated by a brief look at an unusual attempt to present the "physical" body in Victorian literature. In Charlotte Brontë's *Jane Eyre,* Jane's description of Mr. Rochester on the occasion of their second meeting anatomizes him in considerable detail: "I knew my traveller with his broad and jetty eyebrows; his square forehead, made squarer by the horizontal sweep of his black hair. I recognized his decisive nose, more remarkable for character than beauty; his full nostrils, denoting, I thought, choler; his grim mouth, chin, and jaw—yes, all three were very grim, and no mistake. His shape . . . harmonised in squareness with his physiognomy; I suppose it was a good figure in the athletic sense of the term—broad chested and thin flanked, though neither tall nor graceful" (Brontë [1847] 1960, 123). Given Jane's belief in the science of physiognomy, some of the physical details here—the nose in particular—are clearly intended to represent Rochester's nature, but the function of others (the forehead, the chest) would seem to be primarily mimetic, to establish a "physical reality" for the character, a corporeal basis for "Mr. Rochester." As Jane's attention to Rochester's "flanks" suggests, her portrait of Rochester is also vaguely eroticized. It becomes apparent that Rochester's body is doubly sexual, serving as the locus of the character's own sexuality and as a source of erotic fascination for others. Rochester's body does not "mean" anything but simply exists as the untropable physical basis of Jane's (and perhaps Brontë's) sexual attraction to him.

If, unlike Brontë, Dickens seeks to erase the "physical" dimension of his characters precisely as a means of evading the erotic, there is then no basis for identity that exists prior to representation, and individual identity often becomes a free-floating construct in the novel. Thus *Bleak House* is filled with characters who elect to "sign" themselves, to control their representation by constructing their own ex-centric identities as imitations of others. In the opening pages of the novel, the reader is informed that "Conversation Kenge" has "formed himself on the model of a great lord who was his client" (37). Like the notion of legal representation, in which one person "stands" for another, identity among the practitioners of the law would seem to be a matter of defining oneself as a re-presentation of someone else. Just as Guppy models his conversation on "forensic principles," he also increasingly comes to imitate Kenge, and Guppy has his own imitator in Bart Smallweed: "To become a Guppy is the object of his ambition. He dresses at that gentleman (by whom he is patronized), talks at him, walks at him, founds himself entirely on him" (284–85). Initially, this would seem to be part of Dickens's satire on the legal profession, until one realizes that such manipulations are not confined to the novel's lawyers. Skimpole presents himself as a "mere child" in order to evade responsibility, and Bucket, the novel's hero, is so effective as a detective precisely because of his skill at manipulating his self-representations. Arriving at the shooting gallery disguised as a doctor, "a very respectable old gentleman with grey hair, wearing spectacles, and dressed in a black spencer and gaiters and a broad-brimmed hat, and carrying a large gold-headed cane" (358), Bucket enacts the incorporeality that allows the shifting self-representations of the novel: "The physician stopped, and taking off his hat, appeared to vanish by magic and to leave another and quite a different man in his place" (359).

Dickens would seem to be aware that the dematerialization of his characters begins a play of representations that makes identity increasingly problematic in the novel, for the work presents a basis for defining identity that is, in fact, centered on the body. The principle that "true" identity is determined by physical resemblance to one's relatives is most clearly articulated in the case of that other lost child of the narrative: Mr. George. George speculates that "likenesses run in families" (849), and the novel would seem to confirm it. Mr. George and Mr. Rouncewell are "very like each other, sitting face to face," and George's nephew resembles George's own younger self. By the same token, the physical similarity of Esther and Lady Dedlock prompts numerous characters to investigate the relationship between the two women, and the mystery of Esther's identity is finally solved by reference to "identity," her likeness to Lady Dedlock.

Even the physical likeness of mother and daughter, however, is not entirely unproblematic as a means of determining identity. Presented with a seemingly endless procession of veiled female figures, Jo's confusion signals the difficulty. When he is asked by Tulkinghorn to decide if Hortense, dressed in the veil, bonnet, and gown that Lady Dedlock borrowed from her, is the woman he led to the cemetery, Jo identifies the clothing but notes that the hand and voice are different. He concludes that "it is her and it an't her" (326). Initially, Jo's testimony would seem to establish the body as the true basis of identity, his references to the hand and voice allowing Tulkinghorn to penetrate Lady Dedlock's disguise and arrive at the real identity of the figure Jo encountered. The same principle, presented in reverse, operates later in the narrative when Jo meets Esther. Jo notes that her clothing is different from that of the lady he conducted to the graveyard but that Esther looks like "t'other one" (439), and he later refers to Esther as "the lady as wos and yit as warn't the t'other lady" (651). This is yet another assertion in the novel that the bodies of Lady Dedlock and Esther are evidence of their relation, although the similarity of the terms in which Jo conflates Lady Dedlock not only with Esther but with Hortense should give us pause.

The problem is that the very principle of identifying the self by reference to the other threatens the notion of a coherent self-enclosed identity in the first place. All these ladies both are and are not the other lady, as is suggested by the numerous readings of the novel that identify Hortense as a projection of Lady Dedlock's suppressed aggression or Lady Dedlock as an enactment of Esther's repressed sexuality.[11] The ways in which the novel's women continually represent each other thus imply that physical likeness itself serves less to establish identity than to shatter it. Upon first seeing Lady Dedlock, Esther is reminded of the old days at her godmother's when she used to look in her mirror. If Lady Dedlock's face is a mirror for Esther, however, it is a highly unsatisfactory one. Like Lacan's mirror stage, in which the image of the unified self is problematic precisely because it exists outside the self, Lady Dedlock's face serves as a "broken glass" for Esther (262), recalling "scraps" of the past, fragments of her earlier self that leave her "fluttered and troubled." Nor does it seem incidental that Esther finally speculates here not on her own likeness to Lady Dedlock as a key to her identity but on the resemblance between Lady Dedlock and Miss Barbary, a specula(riza)tion that serves less to establish identity through genetic similarity than to problematize the self by multiplying identifications. Thus when Esther notes that Lady Dedlock's voice brings before her mind "innumerable pictures of myself" (266), the stress falls finally not on "myself," on Esther's discovery of her identity, but on the multiple pictures, the fragmentation and dispersal of identity defined through the other.

THE BODY OF THE TEXT

If the body is suppressed in the novel because it is the site of the sexual impulses that serve to shatter identity, this suppression duplicates the difficulties that result from the novel's erasure of sexuality. On the one hand, narrative denial of the body removes the physical basis of identity, turning it into a play of representations. On the other hand, reference to the body, to the physical similarity that suggests one's identity, also problematizes the self. As is the case with sexuality, both repression and revelation of the body endanger identity. Sexuality and the body thus pose problems not only for the characters, who seek a ground on which to establish identity, but for Dickens as well, for the fate of the body in the novel suggests the central tension between sexuality and representation with which Dickens struggles.

As I argued in chapter 1, the sexual resists and disrupts any attempt to represent it. A field of incoherent drives, pulsions, and impulses played out within and through the body, sexuality can be spoken only through what Leo Bersani has called a "narrativization," a rationalization and representation of the sexual that renders it coherent, making it safe for discourse (1986, 40). It is not surprising, then, that sexuality is so literally unspeakable in *Bleak House* and that the difficulties of articulating the mysteries of the sexual are displaced in the novel onto the problems of representing the body, where the sexual is sited/cited. *Yet, even in the form of the primal scene or of the facts of the body, sexuality cannot be represented without becoming something else, something other than sexuality.* Thus the primal scene is a visual experience, a discovery of the mystery of sex. The questions raised by the scene, however, cannot be answered visually, and any linguistic solution must inevitably misunderstand it. As Ned Lukacher has noted, the primal scene is identified precisely by the fact that it has been forgotten, and the truth of reconstructions of the scene must inevitably be "undecidable," suspended between the patient's amnesia and the analyst's imaginative re-creations (1986, 25–31). By the same token, the physical body is, in its materiality, unavailable to narrative. Attempts to represent the body tend to allegorize it, making it mean "personality" or "genetic connection," if nothing else. In a sense, then, it is apt that the problems of sexuality and the body become problems of identity for the characters, for the larger question raised by the novel is also a problem of identity— in a number of senses. The question is not simply what sexuality and the body are, what their "identity" or "nature" is, but whether they are, or can be, "identical" to their representation.[12]

The latter question in particular is the central dilemma of all literature, and Dickens works out a number of answers to the problem. One solution, as we have seen, is simply to acknowledge the limits of representation by refusing to narrate the primal scene between Esther's parents. The very choice of this scene and of Esther's illegitimate birth as the core of the narrative, however, suggests the pressure of the sexual behind the narrative, the insistence that sexuality and the body must be spoken. Thus Dickens displaces the dilemma onto an equally problematic treatment of the body. The problem of representation, however, admits a third solution, which another look at two of the novel's bodies will uncover.

The first body can be said to summarize the difficulties we have just noted. Having accompanied Bucket in his pursuit of Lady Dedlock, Esther describes the end of their journey at the burial ground: "I saw before me, lying on the step, the mother of the dead child. She lay there with one arm creeping round a bar of the iron gate and seeming to embrace it. . . . She lay there a distressed, unsheltered, senseless creature" (814). Because Esther identifies Lady Dedlock by her clothing rather than her body, Esther misrecognizes her identity. Dickens encourages a similar process of misidentification on the part of the reader by having Esther minimize the physical details of the scene in favor of a series of speculations on the connection between the prostrate figure and her mother. In Esther's description the body is replaced by a set of secondary representations ("She who had brought my mother's letter; who could give me the only clue to where my mother was"). Virtually undescribed, the true identity of the body is lost in Esther's meditations on the significance of the figure, recreating in the reader the misrecognition that the exchange of clothes, the shifting representation of identity, has produced in Esther. For both character and reader, the realities of the body and of its identity are lost in a play of signs.

The immediate problem—the mistaking of Lady Dedlock for Jenny—is solved by Esther's final, literal contact with the body: "I lifted the heavy head, put the long dank hair aside, and turned the face. And it was my mother, cold and dead" (814). For the characters, the loss of the body in representation can finally be solved by contact with the body. For Dickens and for the reader, such contact is not possible, although it is surely relevant that the physical description here (of, for example, the "long dank hair") becomes more detailed than usual. How can the body and the identity allied to it be represented without invoking the *glissement* of meaning inherent in representation? The body of Esther's other parent suggests Dickens's solution. This body too is dead, discovered by Tulkinghorn in his rooms at Krook's.

> It is a small room, nearly black with soot, and grease, and dirt. In the rusty skeleton of a grate, pinched at the middle as if poverty had gripped it, a red coke fire burns low. In the corner by the chimney stand a deal table and a broken desk, a wilderness marked with a rain of ink. In another corner a ragged old portmanteau on one of the two chairs serves for cabinet or wardrobe; no larger one is needed, for it collapses like the cheeks of a starved man. The floor is bare, except that one old mat, trodden to shreds of rope-yarn, lies perishing upon the hearth. No curtain veils the darkness of the night, but the discoloured shutters are drawn together, and through the two gaunt holes pierced in them, famine might be staring in—the banshee of the man upon the bed. (150–51)

Once again, as with Lady Dedlock, the body here is given far less attention than is its context, for after this extensive presentation of the room, the body itself is rather cursorily described, and this description keeps moving away from the body to its surroundings: "He lies there, dressed in shirt and trousers, with bare feet. He has a yellow look in the spectral darkness of a candle that has guttered down until the whole length of its wick (still burning) has doubled over and left a tower of winding-sheet above it. His hair is ragged, mingling with his whiskers and his beard—the latter, ragged too, and grown, like the scum and mist around him, in neglect" (151).

Critics of the novel have frequently noted what the last sentence makes obvious: the description serves to displace Nemo into his surroundings, the metonymic linking of character and setting being a favorite device of Dickens. The ultimate significance of the passage, however, is that representation does not work here to disguise or occlude the body but rather to reveal it. If representation of the body always involves a movement away from it, then the passage embraces this tendency, using the representation of setting to detail the nature of the body, which itself cannot be spoken without misrecognition. One realizes also that the speculations that Esther generates over the body at the cemetery work, finally, in a similar way. Ostensibly functioning to further the misidentification of the body as Jenny's, a second glance reveals that such representations also point back to Lady Dedlock, who *did* bring her mother's letter and who *can* furnish a clue to where her mother is. Dickens thus solves the problems of representation by means of representation; if bodies and identities become lost in a play of signs, that very play can be used to articulate them. This solution is used not only to deal with the bodies or identities of individual characters but to answer the larger question of how the body in general and sexuality can be represented. If sexuality is repressed in the novel, Dickens's strategy for resolving this dilemma, for speaking the sexual, thus depends not merely on an acceptance of the *glissements* of language but on nineteenth-century notions of the representational strategies of the repressed body itself. If sex and the body must be signed in narrative, the answers to the problems this raises can be found in the conjunction of signs to form the body of the narrative. Freud was soon to argue that sexual repression leads to the hysterical symptom, in which the body speaks its sexual hopes and fears symbolically. *Bleak House* can be said to reproduce this process isomorphically, the body of this sexually repressed work symbolically encoding the answers not only to the specific mystery of Esther's birth but also to the problem of articulating the larger mystery of the text: sexuality itself.

As Philip Rieff's introduction to *Dora: An Analysis of a Case of Hysteria* suggests, Freud's case history can also be read as a mystery story. Attempting to fathom the "mystery of character," Freud is a "detective of the soul," a sort of spiritual Sherlock Holmes. A "master of detection," Freud must fill in the gaps in the hysteric's narrative and solve the case by piecing Dora's story together from the evidence hidden in her supplementary narratives: the two dreams and her hysterical symptoms (1963, 7–20). Centered, like *Bleak House,* on a young girl whose unwilling complicity in a history of illicit sexuality only gradually becomes known to her, Dora's case engages all of Freud's abilities as a reader, although the text here is not linguistic but somatic: the hysteric body.[13] The hysterical symptom is not only physiological, Freud notes; it also has a "psychical significance, a *meaning*" ([1905] 1961, 40).

Freud continues by elaborating the mechanisms that link the symptom to the unconscious thoughts that determine its meaning. Attempting to interpret Dora's coughing attacks, Freud notes that "it is a rule of psycho-analytic technique that an internal connection which is still undisclosed will announce its presence by means of a contiguity—a temporal proximity—of associations; just as in writing, if 'a' and 'b' are put side by side, it means that the syllable 'ab' is to be formed out of them" (39). The temporal contiguity of Dora's coughing attacks to the absences of Herr K. thus reveals to Freud that Herr K. is the man that Dora "secretly loved." If the hysterical symptom is a form of writing, the rules of reading it are even more complicated than Freud suggests, however, for the construction of the syllable out of the letters is only partially a question of temporal contiguity. In addition, interpretation of the symptom would seem to involve the recognition of spatial contiguity, the placing of the letters "side by side." Freud's readings of the body thus involve not only temporal but physical associations, so that the tickling in Dora's throat suggests, by reason of its proximity to the mouth, a fantasy of oral sexual gratification that is another part of the symptom's meaning.

If the hysteric body can thus be seen as a text whose meanings are revealed by its contiguities, the text of *Bleak House* can be read as a hysteric body. Concealing a sexual meaning centered on a forgotten scene of seduction, *Bleak House* signals its latent sexual content through "symptoms" that can be interpreted by examining the spatial contiguities not of the novel's settings but of the text itself. Such symptoms are particularly evident in the portion of the novel presented by the omniscient narrator and extend beyond the standard Dickensian device of displacing characters into their surroundings. At crucial points in the narrative, the narrator will present a sort of rhetorical flourish, such as his meditation on the body of Nemo: "If this forlorn man could have been prophetically seen lying here by the mother at whose breast he nestled, a little child, with eyes upraised to her loving face, and soft hand scarcely knowing how to close upon the neck to which it crept, what an impossibility the vision would have seemed! Oh, if in brighter days the now-extinguished fire within him ever burned for one woman who held him in her heart, where is she, while these ashes are above ground!" (164). Ostensibly a fairly typical example of Victorian sentiment, this aside is not as innocent as it seems.

To begin with, the passage itself encodes an answer to the mystery of Nemo, who, we are told a few pages earlier, leaves "no more track behind him that any one can trace than a deserted infant" (159). [14] Revolving around the images of man, woman, and child, the passage contains the answers to Nemo's identity and to the central mystery of the novel: the relation of Nemo, Lady Dedlock, and Esther. The narrator hints here at the two crucial scenes that do not, in fact, occur in *Bleak House* but that nonetheless would explain Esther's story: the mother holding the child and the embrace of the young lovers. Although displaced and reversed (Nemo is portrayed here as the infant rather than as the father; the maternal scene comes before the romantic one), the passage would seem to mark a "return of the repressed," suggesting Nemo's paternity of Esther to the careful reader. The aside, however, does not simply hint at the answer to the specific mystery of Esther's origin. It also indirectly reintroduces the elements suppressed in the novel as a whole. Thus the passage stresses the bodies of mother and child and their physical contact, and the sources of sentimentality here, the appeal to maternal and romantic love, are themselves a metonymic displacement of the sexual and biological processes excluded from the novel. The narrative aside, like the symptom of the hysteric, allows Dickens not only to hint at the answers to the novel's mysteries but to speak, however indirectly, the sexuality erased from the novel.

Nemo is not the only character to be presented in this way. As one would expect, Lady Dedlock is also surrounded textually by a series of rhetorical questions. As she gazes into the fire, the narrator asks: "In search of what? Of any hand that is no more, of any hand that never was, of any touch that might have magically changed her life? Or does she listen to the Ghost's Walk and think what step does it most resemble? A man's? A woman's? The pattering of a little child's feet, ever coming on—on—on?" (409). Here again, the elements of the mystery—the interrelation of a man, a woman, and a child and, more broadly, of man, woman, and child—are presented as rhetorical questions, as *the* questions of the narrative. Even before Esther literally makes the echoes of the Ghost's Walk resonate, the narrator's question thus suggests Lady Dedlock's relation to the novel's wandering child. The touch referred to here once again recalls the lost scenes of the novel: the touch of Nemo (the hand that is no more) during the primal scene excised from the novel and the touch of the infant Esther (according to Miss Barbary, the hand that never was). Less graphically than the narrative effusion surrounding Nemo, the passage nonetheless encodes a solution to the central mystery of the novel and reintroduces the physicality, centered here on the touch, suppressed in the narrative. Like the hysterical body, the hidden truths of the novel are displayed across its surface, in its style.

THE EROTICS OF DETECTION

Bleak House thus deals with the difficulties of representing the sexual by recourse to the very metonymies and *glissements* of meaning that make representation so problematic. As Freud suggests, however, the meanings of the hysteric body do not end with the representation of sex; they also act as a substitute for sexual satisfaction. Although Freud does not seem to realize it fully, this means that the symptom not only has a sexual meaning but also enacts sexuality. The confusion is evident in Freud's statement that "a symptom signifies the representation—the realization—of a phantasy with a sexual content, that is to say, it signifies a sexual situation" ([1905] 1961, 47). Moving from the idea of representation to the notion of realization, Freud immediately elides the latter perception, concluding that the symptom "signifies" sex. "Realization," however, suggests that the symptom *is* sex, an enactment of it, just as, Freud later argued in "Some General Remarks on Hysterical Attacks," the cognitive "absence" experienced during the hysterical fit enacts the loss of consciousness during coitus ([1909] 1961, 233). Like the symptomatic body of the hysteric, the textual body of *Bleak House* itself "realizes" the sexuality that is suppressed at its core. This sexuality occurs most clearly in the novel in the process of detection and interpretation, which produces—and transforms—sexuality for both the characters and the reader.[15]

In effect, the novel anticipates Marie Bonaparte's troping of detective fiction, and detection itself, as a substitute for childhood investigations of sex, attempts to uncover and explain the primal scene (1935, 259–93).[16] From this perspective, knowledge is always, implicitly, sexual knowledge, and as a result, the exchange of knowledge is an erotic interaction. In his analysis of Dora, Freud is not finally concerned to determine what Dora knows about sex (since he soon concludes that she knows everything) but to uncover the source of her information. Dora's knowledge, he decides, came from her conversations with Frau K., and he asserts that Frau K. is the ultimate object of Dora's affections because the intimate conversations between the two women are erotic not only in their content but in their form, an "oral intercourse" that realizes Dora's deepest desires. Freud is aware that his own conversations with Dora about sex, his attempts to "penetrate" her secrets, enact a similar erotic intimacy, a fact that he strenuously, and unconvincingly, tries to dismiss (Hertz 1985, 234).

A similar sexuality of knowing pervades *Bleak House*. The case of Tulkinghorn's murder aside, most of the novel's detectives seek to unravel sexual secrets such as Lady Dedlock's relation to Hawdon or, in the case of Mrs. Snagsby, Mr. Snagsby's supposed infidelities, but it is not only the content of the mysteries that links knowledge to sexuality. Tulkinghorn's investigations, his desire for power over Lady Dedlock, would seem finally to derive from displaced eroticism, particularly since his actions are mirrored by Guppy, whose express purpose is to win Esther's hand and whose discoveries enact the intimate knowledge of Esther that is his goal. If the motives of detection are thus often sexual in *Bleak House,* the intimacy of shared knowledge is itself eroticized in the novel, even when the secret is not itself sexual. This is nowhere clearer than in the case of Bucket, who gets into bed with Mrs. Bucket and, stuffing a sheet into her mouth so that she can't utter "a word of surprise," proceeds to—tell her his suspicions about Hortense. Bucket's confrontation with Hortense in front of Sir Leicester underscores the erotic connection that his knowledge of Hortense's secret creates. Seated on the sofa arm in arm with her, Bucket responds to Hortense's calling him "my angel" by referring to her as "darling," and he conveys her to the police station by "enfolding and pervading her like a cloud, and hovering away with her as if he were a homely Jupiter and she the object of his affections" (746).

This sexuality of detection applies not only to the characters but to the reader, for reading the novel also involves the discovery of intimate information, although the latent eroticism of reading is not itself directly expressed in *Bleak House*. Displaced and modified, however, the sexuality of reading would seem to inform Esther's remarks near the conclusion of her narrative: "The few words that I have to add to what I have written are soon penned; then I and the unknown friend to whom I write will part for ever. Not without much dear remembrance on my side. Not without some, I hope, on his or hers" (877). Rewritten here as the intimacy of friendship, the relation of writer and reader or text and reader, the sharing of Esther's secrets seems intended precisely to provoke "dear remembrance," to institute an emotional bond. This address to the audience, the only occasion on which Esther even hints at the motives for her "portion of these pages," suggests that Esther's self-disclosure is intended to "win some love to herself" from the reader. Just as Esther suppresses any mention of her sexual desires within the narrative, the erotic component of this interaction with the reader is repressed, rewritten as the (projected) memory of an emotional tie. With its fond memories of revelations and intimacies, reaching the conclusion of the novel is not, finally, all that different from the end of a long affair.

Esther's remark, however, suggests a necessary refinement of our analysis, for the intimacy of the exchange of knowledge during reading cannot be mutual. If the friend to whom Esther writes is "unknown," Esther cannot then experience any genuine "remembrance" of him or her. The erotics of reading thus cannot be modeled on intersubjectivity, on a mutual interchange between text and reader, but rather on the text as an object of knowledge. A look back at the examples of intimacy cited above suggests that, like reading, detection and interpretation are always one-sided. Thus Tulkinghorn learns Lady Dedlock's secret while remaining mysterious to her, just as Bucket knows Hortense while being enigmatic himself. In the exchange of knowledge, information circulates in one direction, and the implicit sexual relation that results is marked by an imbalance of power. Pervading and enfolding Hortense, Bucket does not merely penetrate and surround her but also enacts the ontological and epistemological superiority of Jupiter. Hortense is only "the object of his affections."

As the latter example suggests, the detective or interpreter is implicitly gendered here as male. Just as Freud is concerned to insist on his status as the knowing subject and on Dora's role as the object of interpretation, whose own knowledge is, at best, false or unconscious, Dickens would seem to regard knowledge as a masculine province. The death of Nemo early in the novel means that the majority of the novel's secrets are held by women (Lady Dedlock, Miss Barbary, Hortense) and that the majority of the novel's detectives are men (Tulkinghorn, Bucket, Guppy, Mr. Smallweed). The major exception to this principle proves the rule: Mrs. Snagsby's attempts to penetrate Mr. Snagsby's supposed sexual secret are wrong, both in the assumption that Snagsby has such a secret and that a woman could correctly interpret it.[17] Thus, despite Esther's notion that the reader may be either a him or a her, the implied reader who probes and analyzes the textual body of *Bleak House* is always male, regardless of his or her biological gender.

Dickens's gendering of the detective-reader is important because it implies a particular model of interpretation and of reading, a masculine epistemology of detection. As Toril Moi notes, in Freud's analysis of Dora, the male symbol of knowledge is the penis, which implies a truth that is whole and complete in contrast to the sort of knowledge represented by Dora: fragmentary, diffuse, and unfinished (1985, 196). Such assumptions are not alien to Dickens, for if Bucket continually shakes his forefinger at Hortense during the climactic scene noted above, this is because Bucket, as the novel's true detective, has his "powers of penetration" repeatedly summarized by the synecdoche of this phallic forefinger, the symbol of the intersection of knowledge, power, and the erotic. It is this male model of detection, with its stress not only on the erotic domination of the object of scrutiny but also on the completeness of knowledge, that suggests how the dangers of sexuality in *Bleak House* can be overcome.

Bucket can be seen as a masculine fantasy figure who counters the anxiety over the fragmentation of the self produced by sexuality. To begin with, Bucket seems to know everything, to represent a knowledge that is itself complete. This pansophism is symbolically confirmed when he identifies Hortense as the murderess because the wadding of the gun used to shoot Tulkinghorn is part of a printed description of Chesney Wold. Literally bringing together the parts of that text, Bucket presents the "whole truth," a truth exemplified by his own narrative of the murder, in which there are no gaps or aporia.[18] Based on the symbolic wholeness of the phallus, this unified knowledge implies, in turn, the completeness and coherence of the knowing (male) subject. Thus, despite his ability to "pervade" a "vast number of houses and . . . an infinity of streets" and his protean talent for creating various self-representations, Bucket's identity is unified by an "undercurrent of forefinger" (716), by his identity as a detective. Even when he is disguised, for example, as a doctor, Bucket nonetheless signals this identity by carrying a gold-headed cane, a representation of the forefinger-phallus that signals Bucket's status as the integral subject, the *one* who knows. If both sexuality and its repression shatter the self in *Bleak House,* the erotics of detection provide a solution to the problem. Enacting sexuality in the form of interpretation, the detective not only avoids the dissolution of the self but experiences an eroticism that reinforces identity: the identity of the detective.

As such, Bucket provides a model for the (implicitly male) reader's own eroticized probing of the body of the novel.[19] Not only encountering sexual secrets but "realizing" the sexual in the intimacy of interpretation, the reader remains unscathed, his identity as interpreter not only intact but reinforced by the mechanisms of reading. The process of reading the novel also serves to transform the text, which, based on a repressed sexual secret, itself poses a problem of "identity." Divided into two narratives, *Bleak House* is, at any given point in the reading, always other than itself. Creating a knowledge that is complete by discovering the secrets of the text and by imaginatively linking the two halves of the narration (and, with the first readers of the novel, unifying the parts of the serially published work), the reader not only constructs a coherent narrative and confers a unified "identity," a meaning, on the work but, in the process, implies the power of reason over the drives and impulses that fragment the characters.

In *The Hound of the Baskervilles,* Sherlock Holmes explains detection: "It is the scientific use of the imagination, but we have always some material basis on which to start our speculation" (Doyle [1902] 1963, 38). If, for Dickens, the greatest mysteries are the secrets of biology, of sexuality and the body, representation must inevitably dematerialize these entities, falsifying the speculations. The answer lies, *Bleak House* suggests, not in the materiality of the body, which cannot be narrated, but in the materiality of the sign, in the "body" of the text that the reader encounters. Just as Dickens solves the problems of representing sexuality, the impossibility and yet the necessity of speaking it, by embracing the metonymies of representation, the reader, like Bucket, solves the problems experienced by the characters, who are threatened both by the sexual and by its repression. Enacting sexuality in the process of interpretation, the reader both experiences and transforms the sexual, controlling its tendency to scatter and fragment the self and the text. The problematics of the representation of the sexual, the problems of sexuality, are redeemed in *Bleak House* by the sexuality of representation.

Dickens's manipulation of representation anticipates the aestheticism of the fin de siècle, the self-conscious textuality of Oscar Wilde. Concerned, like Dickens, with the effects of sexuality on the self and focused, like Austen, on sexual desire, Wilde both summarizes and extends the reasons for Victorian sexual anxiety. Writing during the period when the newly constructed concept of homosexuality was producing a reorganization of nineteenth-century conceptions of sex, Wilde recapitulates the sexual anxieties of the writers who preceded him. Projecting the antitaxonomic and destabilizing properties previously attributed to sexuality in general onto the idea of homoerotic desire, *The Picture of Dorian Gray* not only demonstrates the dangers posed by the sexual to the social structure or the self but also illustrates an anxiety that is latent in the works of Austen, Gaskell, and Dickens: the fear that sex and sexuality will cause the disintegration of the novel itself. Wilde's novel not only articulates this threat but enacts it; finally, his techniques for restraining the anarchic potential of homosexual desire fail, and the novel collapses into incoherence. The epitome of the reasons for Victorian sexual anxiety, Wilde's novel ultimately looks forward as well. If Austen institutes the erotic discretion of Victorian fiction through the construction of the linked notions of personal and textual "repression," Wilde reverses the process, his presentation of a "de-repressed" desire foreshadowing a radically different, modern response to the problems of sexual representation.

CHAPTER 5

"The Perfect Type of the Perfect Pleasure": Homosexual Desire in *The Picture of Dorian Gray*

We will probably never know exactly what happened on the evening, just over a hundred years ago, when Robert Ross seduced Oscar Wilde. Even less clear than the details of Wilde's introduction to homosexual praxis, however, is the question of how Wilde's homosexuality is to be interpreted, how it can be situated in relation to his psychology, or to his art, or even to our understanding of homosexuality itself. In his recent biography of Wilde, Richard Ellmann attempts to elucidate some of these difficulties. Wilde's involvement with Ross, Ellmann argues, was "perhaps" motivated by "curiosity or caprice," although it may have also stemmed from his desire for a secret life (1988, 275). Ellmann thus provides homosexuality with a curious etiology, at least in Wilde's case. Given the growth of homophobia at the end of the last century (Sedgwick 1985, 201; Weeks 1977, 15; Dellamora 1990, 194), caprice or curiosity seems an insufficient reason for Wilde to adopt a highly dangerous mode of behavior, and the desire for a secret life might certainly have taken other, more innocuous forms. Moreover, Ellmann's qualifying "perhaps" serves finally to reinscribe the origins of homosexual desire under the sign of the ineffable.

However obscure its origins, homoeroticism has striking effects in Ellmann's view. Homosexual love, he continues, roused Wilde from "pasteboard conformity to the expression of latent desires" (278), most notably the desire to think of himself as a criminal. The crime of forgery, in particular, impressed Wilde as an apt metaphor for his social self-presentation because he was "now in league with the underworld of people who pretended to be what they were not, like some group of Masons without the law" (299). We are apparently not to lament Wilde's decision, however, for this "new" sexual direction "liberated" Wilde's art, providing a "freshness" that suggests that "running foul of the law in his sexual life" stimulated his thought on "every subject" (286).

As tropes of the unspeakable, the figures of homosexual desire informing Ellmann's discussion are finally as familiar as the Romantic image of the outcast artist upon which his analysis is ultimately predicated. The association of the homosexual and the criminal, the assumption around which Ellmann's discussion of the effects of homosexuality revolves, was current in Wilde's own era, and it is itself the product of an assumption that the homosexual not only runs foul of the law in his sexual life but runs foul of the laws of sexual life. Thus Wilde's trials and imprisonment are the seemingly inevitable material result of his violation of a set of more abstract laws: the "laws of nature." If homosexual desire is seen as a force beyond such natural laws, this desire demonstrates, in Ellmann's presentation, its own baroque physics, the central principle of which would seem to be internal contradiction. Homosexuality is, for Ellmann, apparently both choice and compulsion. Arising out of "caprice" and producing a "new" sexuality, it is nonetheless the expression of "latent desires," if only the desire for criminality. Moreover, arising from a whim, homosexuality would seem to epitomize the unstable, mutable nature of all sexual desire. Once it is aroused, however, such mutability ends, and homosexual desire becomes unalterable. Once Wilde had experienced homosexual love, Ellmann notes, "the serious embrace of women was forbidden him" (278).

What is finally most striking about Ellmann's discussion of homosexual desire, however, is not that it is contradictory or that it reflects a set of covert popular assumptions but that there is room in it for virtually everything *but* desire. Situated in a series of contexts—psychological, social, artistic—Wilde's homosexuality is considered in every light but the most obvious one. Either as cause or effect of Wilde's seduction by Ross, homoerotic desire is actually absent from Ellmann's account; the only real desires here are an attraction to the illicit or to a secret existence. Homosexuality, it would seem, really *is* unspeakable. This absence at the heart of Ellmann's discussion is not merely coincidental, however; rather, it is the (il)logical consequence of his assumptions. Perceived as outside of both the juridical precepts of culture and the "laws of nature," homosexuality would seem to resist the symbolization of language itself, remaining incoherent. Because it exists, however, it must finally enter discourse. Ellmann's solution to the resulting dilemma—the impossibility and yet the necessity of articulating this desire—is aptly summarized, in fact, by the image of the Masonic confraternity of the sexual criminal. Just as the Masonic "order" is not chaotic but consists of rites that are "unspeakable," hidden from the uninitiated to whom they must remain mysterious, so the mystery of homosexual desire is both ineffable and yet presumed to follow its own set of covert laws. Ellmann thus inscribes the incoherence of homosexuality in the contradictions of his text and yet relies on a set of covert reifications of "homosexuality" (the criminal, the "unnatural"), which give form to the chaotic and elide the incomprehensibility of homosexual desire.

The difficulties of articulating "the love that dare not speak its name" are not Ellmann's alone. A sense of homosexuality as incoherent not only animates contemporary discussions of the subject but also informs Wilde's own work. As we shall see, *The Picture of Dorian Gray* reveals Wilde's struggle to represent the delights and dangers of sexual desire, and although the desire it explores is, at least implicitly, homosexual, Wilde's novel is perhaps the epitome of the nineteenth-century novel's battle with the sexual in general. Because homosexuality is seen by the late Victorians as the purest example of the difficulties of all sexuality, of its anarchic potential and uncodifiability, *Dorian Gray* illustrates the impossibility of either expressing or avoiding the sexual. Wilde's novel does not merely represent these difficulties, however. Finally, it enacts them. Ultimately, Wilde's strategies for the management or restraint of sexual desire fail, the work is unable to control its representation of the sexual, and the novel itself dissolves into the incoherence that is the focus of nineteenth-century sexual anxiety.

Homosexual Desire in *The Picture of Dorian Gray*

In order to understand Wilde's presentation of sexual desire, we must first look at the recodification and restructuring of sex and sexuality that took place during the last quarter of the nineteenth century. As Foucault has argued, it is during this period that "perversion" is implanted in the individual, that earlier notions of sodomy as a set of vaguely defined sexual actions, potential disorders in the sexuality of all humans, are replaced by a stress on the actor. Crystallized within the individual by medical and psychological discourses, "homosexuality" appears as a particular vice of certain people, which allows the gradual creation of a "homosexual" identity based on nonsexual as well as sexual behaviors (Foucault 1978, 42–44).[1] Foucault stresses the contemporary articulation of this identity as "inversion," the idea that the homosexual male represents a woman's soul trapped in a man's body, but as Eve Sedgwick has recently argued, the period is marked by a number of competing definitional models. Most notably, the idea of inversion is balanced by a definition of *homosexuality* as same-sex object choice, the definition implicitly assumed by Wilde (Sedgwick 1990, 157–58, 160).[2]

Under either definition, the emergence of a discourse of the homoerotic reorganized the conceptual field in which it appeared, so that the idea of homosexuality redefined—in a sense created—the notion of heterosexuality.[3] The result is not only a new organization of "sex" as a cultural idea but also a redistribution of the symbolic meanings of the sexual. For our purpose, the importance of this new ideological configuration is its reworking of nineteenth-century understandings of the chaos associated with the sexual, a re-vision that has been clarified by Guy Hocquenghem. Sexual desire, Hocquenghem argues, is merely an undifferentiated polyvocal flux that is arbitrarily divided by culture into heterosexual and homosexual drives (1978, 36). Homosexual desire thus becomes the unclassifiable residue left over after the strictly defined, socially prescribed form of desire, the heterosexual, is constructed. As a result, the polymorphous, unfixed qualities of all sexual desire are projected onto homosexual desire, which comes to serve as the chaotic, ineffable Other of heterosexual desire. If, as we have seen, the chaotic "nature" of sexuality, including sexual desire, is itself a Victorian belief (albeit one that persists in certain forms to the present day), Hocquenghem accurately reveals how the development of the notion of homosexuality realigned contemporary sexual meanings.

This realignment does not end with the articulation of homosexuality as the locus of sexual chaos (an idea doubtless both confirmed and reinforced by competing definitions of the homoerotic). Even constructed as the Other of heterosexuality, Hocquenghem notes, "the emergence of unformulated desire is too destructive to be allowed to become more than a fleeting phenomenon which is immediately surrendered to a recuperative interpretation" (80). Even as homosexuality is defined as chaotic and excluded from Western culture's self-definition, normative perceptions of it thus are created that attempt to delimit its anarchic potential and its incoherence by reading it in relation to heterosexuality, a dual movement that we have already seen at work in Ellmann. This is clearest in the inversion model, which simultaneously stresses the alarming erasure of gender difference (a woman's soul in a man's body) and recuperates that difference by invoking Cartesian dualism: the (female) soul versus the (male) body. Moreover, the idea of inversion implicitly insists that desire is always heterosexual, a relation of "male" and "female" elements, an insistence that is finally apparent in the assumption that questions of sexuality *must be* related to ideas of gender difference in the first place. Posited as Other to the heterosexual, inversion's anarchic implications are thus restrained by its assimilation to heterosexuality.

In contrast to the inversion model, the chaotic implications of the idea of homosexuality as same-sex desire are controlled, not by assimilation, but, more subtly, by its definition *against* heterosexuality. In effect, this means that same-sex male desire is articulated in opposition to the symbolic dominance of the phallus, the only sexual organ that really exists in Oedipal heterosexuality (Hocquenghem 1978, 81). The signifier par excellence, the phallus serves to organize and structure numerous aspects of the sexual realm: it provides a focal point, and hence an organization, for the male erotic body; it implies a hierarchical structure for sexual relations in which individuals are divided into two groups: those who have the phallus (men) and those who desire it (women); and it allows a codification of the otherwise ineffable sensations of sexual pleasure, which are focused on the male orgasm.

Seen from this perspective, homosexuality is constructed precisely as a threat to the structures of (Oedipal) heterosexuality. To begin with, same-sex sexual activity decenters the erotic body by introducing a second potential site of pleasure, the anus, which not only challenges the hegemony of the phallus in the symbolic organization of the body but also recalls the term suppressed by such an organization, the "other" genitalia—the *vagina*.[4] By the same token, the possibility of nonphallic pleasure threatens the easy codification of sexual experience, reintroducing the possibility of an ineffable nonorgasmic sexual satisfaction. Finally, possessor of the phallus, the homosexual is seen as perverse because he nonetheless desires the phallus. In the gender ideology of Western culture, he is a (male) subject who dreams of becoming a (female) object. As such, the homosexual desires to be an artificial woman, which is to say an image of an image, since woman herself is a phallocentric construction who functions only as an object in the sexual economy. Seen as same-sex object choice, homosexuality is thus defined by Western culture as chaotically polymorphous in relation to the phallic organization of heterosexuality. Although this definition once again contains the ineffability of homosexuality by assimilating it to normative heterosexual models (in, for example, the implicit gendering of subject/object relations), its overall mechanism is more subtle: it produces homosexuality as polymorphous and chaotic in order to insist on the structures of (ordered) heterosexual desire.[5]

Such an analysis would not have consciously occurred to Wilde, who wrote from within these structures at precisely the point that they were produced, and whose own writing is in fact part of their production. Wilde implicitly assumes this construction, however, seeing same-sex object choice (the definition of homosexuality that, following Wilde, I will hereafter employ) as inherently chaotic. As such, Wilde's novel illustrates fin-de-siècle notions of the homoerotic as "in-different," as incompatible with some of the distinctions that ground Victorian perceptions. Although homosexuality was associated with the erasure not only of gender but also of class boundaries, Wilde's concern is finally with psychic rather than social chaos, with the effects of homosexual desire on the distinctions of subject and object and self and other. Moreover, because homosexuality is constructed as the Other of heterosexuality, as the place where the chaotic potential of the sexual is abjected, *The Picture of Dorian Gray* also provides the perfect summary of Victorian notions of the chaotic nature of the sexual in general and uncovers an anxiety that is latent in Austen, Gaskell, and Dickens. Ultimately, this anxiety is not a question of difference but of meaning, of the actual difficulty of representing sexuality. As we shall see, Wilde's novel reveals the anxiety that the homoerotic (and hence the erotic per se) not only cannot be contained by the representational structures of fiction but that it can destroy the novel itself.

HOMOEROTICISM AND THE DISPERSAL OF THE SELF

Since the appearance of Charles Whibley's review in the *Scots Observer* calling the novel suited for none but "outlawed noblemen and perverted telegraph boys," critics have almost universally identified a homosexual subtext in *Dorian Gray*.[6] Wilde does not overtly articulate the relations between the novel's three central males as homosexual, yet even to the casual reader the affinities between Dorian, Lord Henry, and Basil seem to extend beyond the homosocial ties of male bonding. A closer look at the work reveals that the relations of the male characters initiate a complex descent into the unstructured, a dissolution of the distinction of subject and object and of self and other that strongly suggests the polymorphous tendencies and decentering of the self that Wilde associated with homoerotic impulses. Wilde's presentation of male interaction focuses on two related phenomena: an emphasis on the visual, which ultimately reveals the desiring subject's simultaneous status as desired object; and the use of metaphors of fluidity and interfusion to define a concept of "influence," a dissolution of the boundaries of self and other. Ultimately, *Dorian Gray* depicts Wilde's sense of the disintegrative effects of the homoerotic desire that can operate under cover of homosocial bonding.

As befits a novel that opens in an artist's studio, Wilde's presentation of male relations begins with the complexities of vision, with Basil's explanation of the impact that Dorian has had on his art. For Basil, Dorian's mere "visible presence" has defined the possibility of an entirely new artistic manner. As Basil notes, he now "sees things differently" and is able to perceive in a "plain woodland" the wonder he has "always looked for" (Wilde [1891]

1968, 18). Initially, such a discussion establishes a set of implicit ontological positions. Here Basil is the viewing subject, Dorian the suggestive object. As Freud pointed out, however, and Wilde realizes, the moment such positions are established, they allow the possibility of a reversal. The viewing subject can himself be a viewed object, and the dominance and control implied by the act of seeing can give way to the passivity and submission of being seen. In fact, this reversal would seem to be Basil's chief fear, for the portrait of Dorian is, Basil notes, also a portrait of Basil's own "soul," reflecting his idolatry of Dorian. Consequently, he cannot bring himself to exhibit the portrait: "The world might guess it; and I will not bare my soul to their shallow, prying eyes. My heart shall never be put under their microscope. There is too much of myself in the thing, Harry—too much of myself!" (19).

Basil's anxiety here would seem to stem from two related difficulties: the transformation of his "soul" into an object viewed by the public and the additional revelation of his loss of self in his idolatry of Dorian. As it happens, the curious reversibility of Basil's status as viewing subject and viewed object in relation to the portrait merely re-creates his first meeting with Dorian himself, an encounter that Basil describes as being almost entirely visual. At a crush at Lady Brandon's, Basil becomes subliminally aware that someone is looking at him and turns to see Dorian Gray. Basil's positioning here, first as object and then as subject, is summarized by the next "move": Basil's and Dorian's eyes meet. Although he is simultaneously subject and object, Basil's reaction is a fear of his reduction solely to the status of an object, a fear based on the perception that Dorian is so "fascinating" that he could absorb Basil's "whole nature." Attempting to flee, Basil is stopped by Lady Brandon, who introduces him to her guests one by one until he finds himself "face to face" with Dorian, and their eyes meet again. An introduction to Dorian, Basil later concludes, was "inevitable" (15).

Originating in a visual encounter and eventuating in a visual object, the portrait, Basil and Dorian's relation demonstrates the continual reversibility of the positions of subject and object in the scopic economy. As Basil's fear of being seen, of the "absorption" of his personality by Dorian suggests, a struggle for the status of subject can ensue, and Basil's portrait of Dorian can be read, in part, as Basil's attempt to affirm his position as viewing subject. Ultimately, however, Dorian prevails. The final encounter of the two men begins with Dorian watching Basil "with the passion of a spectator" as Basil looks at the changed picture. Dorian's sense of "triumph" on this occasion is completed by his murder of Basil, by Basil's reduction to a "thing" seated at the attic table (161): a symbolic consummation of Basil's enthrallment by Dorian, of his status as an object. The battle for visual dominance between the two men concludes, appropriately enough, by coming full circle, with Dorian idly sitting down after the murder to sketch faces, only to remark that "every face that he drew seemed to have a fantastic likeness to Basil" (165). The artist has become the aesthetic object, the object has become the artist.

This struggle for dominance, for the status of subject, between males does not simply represent the competitiveness traditionally associated with men, however. Ed Cohen has argued that the visual in *Dorian Gray* is the arena in which Wilde can represent the otherwise unrepresentable—homosexuality. Hence Basil's portrait of Dorian expresses the homoerotic desire traditionally excluded from verbal representation (1987, 806–7). In fact, the visual itself is particularly appropriate to the portrayal of homosexual relations. The potential reversibility of subject and object is implicit in heterosexual relations but is concealed by the cultural construction of woman as viewed object, a construction that establishes and protects the male's status as viewing subject. In homoerotic relations between males, however, this protective barrier does not exist, and the individual is always threatened with the loss of his position as a subject. Sibyl Vane, whose status as an actress confirms her role as object of appreciation, nominally provides the traditional feminine guarantee of male subjectivity in the novel, but as critics have often noted, her place in the narrative is marginal, and as we have seen, male visual activity in the work is more often focused on other men.[7] Transcending simple male bonding, the scopic interactions of the novel's male characters implicitly articulate Wilde's sense of the ontological perils of the homoerotic.

Moreover, as Lacan has suggested, the curious reversibility of the act of seeing is not simply a struggle for visual control. The scopic economy also implies desire. The desire inherent in the viewing subject's visual activity establishes an implicit "other" position, the gaze, which is the possibility of being desired by the other (Davis 1983, 987–88). The look is therefore doubly reversible, implying the transformation of the subject into an object and of the desire for the other into a desire to be desired by the other. This is in fact the basis for the novel's premise: Dorian's wish to change places with the portrait. Awakened by Lord Henry to his youth and beauty, Dorian is asked to come look at "himself," at the completed portrait, and "the sense of his own beauty" comes over him "like a revelation" (32). Situated precisely between his status as subject and object, Dorian implicitly chooses the latter. He is jealous, he says to Basil, of the immortal beauty of art: "I am less to you than your ivory Hermes or your silver Faun. You will like them always. How long will you like me? Till I have my first wrinkle, I suppose. I know, now, that when one loses one's good looks, whatever they may be, one loses everything" (33). Choosing the status of the object, choosing to be desired by the other, Dorian makes his wish to be eternally young and beautiful.

Thus the visual in *Dorian Gray* foregrounds Wilde's sense of the instability of the subject in homosexual relations, and Dorian's selling of his soul in the Faustian bargain that initiates the action of the novel can be seen as the abdication of the status of unselfconscious heterosexual subject. Instead, Dorian experiences the continually shifting positions associated with male homoeroticism, the recurrent transformation of the desiring subject into a desired object. In fact, this ontological instability is summarized by Dorian's own contradictory impulses, his simultaneous wish to dominate Basil visually and yet to be the object of Basil's desire. The novel suggests that homosexual desire is even more complicated than this, however. The precariousness of the homosexual's status as a subject is additionally threatened by the dissolution of the distinction of the self and the other. Presented as a notion of "influence," this dissolution is thematized in the novel by images of the auditory, the olfactory, and the fluid.

Moving beyond mere friendship, the relations of the novel's three main characters are based on a rather curious idea of "influence." Basil's first encounter with Dorian suggests the nature of such influence, since Basil narrates it as a process of self-surrender, as being "absorbed" by Dorian. It is thus not surprising that Lord Henry should define "influence" as the process of giving a person "one's own soul" (24). As it happens, Dorian himself is susceptible to influence. Talking to Dorian as he sits for the portrait, Lord Henry "awakens" him to the "new Hedonism." The process, Lord Henry decides, "was like playing upon an exquisite violin. He answered to every touch and thrill of the bow. There was something terribly enthralling in the exercise of influence. No other activity was like it. To project one's soul into some gracious form, and let it tarry there for a moment; to hear one's own intellectual views echoed back to one with all the added music of passion and youth; to convey one's temperament into another as though it were a subtle fluid or a strange perfume; there was real joy in that" (42).

As the use here of auditory rather than visual metaphors suggests, "influence" does not imply a struggle for domination like that implicit in the scopic economy. Although the notion of Dorian as the instrument upon which Lord Henry plays would seem to suggest such control, a closer look at the metaphor reveals that influence also involves interfusion, the beginning of the dissolution of the boundaries of self and other. Lord Henry's influence is articulated in terms of music not simply because it has been exercised through auditory means, through speech, but also because music (like language) implies the fusion of internal and external. Literally entering the ear, Wilde suggests, sound is simultaneously experienced as inside and outside, as internal and external. Thus the narrator notes that Lord Henry's words touch "some secret chord" in Dorian and seem "to have come really from himself" (26). The auditory is thus the perfect metaphor for Lord Henry's project, for his goal is not merely to "convey his temperament" into Dorian, to make the other into the self, but to hear his views "echoed back" by Dorian, who will have added his own "music" of passion and youth to this shared "soul." Thus Lord Henry himself will be "enthralled," since influence is finally a process of identification. It is in this sense, then, that we are to understand the ending of Lord Henry's meditation on Dorian as an "experiment" or "study." Although his thoughts would seem to suggest that Lord Henry is the detached scientist, his reflections conclude with a strange reversal: "It often happened that when we thought we were experimenting on others we were really experimenting on ourselves" (65). The traditional distinction between the scientist and the experimental subject becomes impossible when the self is identified with the other.

As Eve Sedgwick suggests, homoerotic desire has been defined, since Wilde's era, as involving a confusion between identification with the other man and desire for the other man, and the novel's concept of influence would seem to reflect symbolically Wilde's sense of the homoeroticism of such identification (1985, 105–6; 1990, 159). The additional thematics of perfumes and fluids underscore this notion, implying, like music, that "influence" is a process of interfusion. In the case of the "poisonous" book that leads Dorian deeper into evil, influence is presented as olfactory; a "heavy odor of incense" seems to "cling about [the book's] pages and to trouble the brain" (129), and the interpenetration of Dorian and the text is made particularly clear. The book seems "to contain the story of [Dorian's] own life, written before he had lived it" (130). Presented as the blending of self and other, even of animate and inanimate, the homosocial dissolves in this instance into a coded form of the homosexual, with relations between males, even between male author and reader, seen as the loss of the boundaries of the self, as assimilation with the other. Although this process can be read as a form of symbolic penetration, Dorian's summary of Lord Henry's effect on him suggests a different mechanism: "You filled me with a wild desire to know everything about life. For days after I met you, something seemed to throb in my veins. . . . There was an exquisite poison in the air" (54). Although attributed to the air, the changes in Dorian are actually the result of Lord Henry's "poisonous theories," an influence that is seen less as penetration than as incorporation. Rather than an external force exerted on the body, the throbbing in Dorian's veins suggests the combination of blood and poison, the infusion and assimilation of alien fluid into the body. Defined precisely as desire, as the desire to know about life, Lord Henry's influence on Dorian is seen as the blending of the self and the other.

Influence in *Dorian Gray*, then, does not suggest domination but fluidity, the "flowing in" of the other into the self and a resulting liquidity of identity.[8] Ultimately, however, even the incorporation of external odors and fluids is an inadequate metaphor for Wilde's sense of the homosexual's desiring relation to the world. Although Basil attributes the curious relation between Dorian and his portrait to a "mineral poison" in the paints, Dorian wonders if his link to the portrait involves an even subtler interaction—an atomic link: "Was there some subtle affinity between the chemical atoms, that shaped themselves into form and color on the canvas, and the soul that was within him?" (99). As it happens, Dorian eventually answers his own question, concluding that perhaps "things external to ourselves vibrate in unison with our moods and passions, atom calling to atom in secret love of strange affinity" (110). In effect, this doctrine of atomic affinities serves to erase completely the distinction between the self and anything external to it, to assert the necessary interrelation of all matter, of everything. It is the ultimate figure for Wilde's perception of the nature of homosexual desire, which seeks finally to deny all difference: to return desire to the polymorphous, to dissolve the self, and to fuse the individual with the world. As such, homosexual desire is seen as the continual attempt to reduce the "hetero" to the "homo," the different to the same, a desire summarized in the continual collapse of distinctions in the novel: between inside and outside, art and life, self and other, animate and inanimate, reader and text.

THE DANGERS OF DESIRE

Analyzing Wilde's political writing, Jonathan Dollimore has argued that Wilde embraced the dispersal of the self associated with "deviant desire" (1991, 14), yet *Dorian Gray* suggests a certain anxiety about the dissolution of the subject. If the relations of the male characters in the novel finally articulate the impulses of homosexual desire as a drive toward the unstructured, Wilde clearly indicates the dangers of such desire. Offering Dorian a cigarette, Lord Henry notes that the "cigarette is the perfect type of a perfect pleasure. It is exquisite, and it leaves one unsatisfied. What more can one want?" (84). If one is left unsatisfied, what one always wants, of course, is more. Overtly articulated as a generalized passion for life and for new sensations, desire in the novel is seen as insatiable. The "curiosity about life" that is stirred in Dorian by Lord Henry seems to "increase with gratification," and pleasure, it would seem, is never perfect. The more Dorian experiences, "the more he desired to know. He had mad hungers that grew more ravenous as he fed them" (132). Unlike Austen, however, it is less the notion of desire's insatiability that troubles Wilde than his belief in its tendency to de-realize the individual, both to turn the self into an object and to shatter its coherence. The story of Dorian Gray can be seen as a descent into chaos, a narrative of the dangers of a generalized desire that, conceived as an extension of the polymorphous tendencies of the homoerotic, has disastrous effects on the self.

To begin with, *Dorian Gray* is replete with the imagery of the automaton, from the "things" that Dorian encounters at the opium parlor to the "monstrous marionettes" making "gestures like live things" silhouetted against the window shades of the East End (187). Desire, it would seem, reduces the human to the nonhuman. As the narrator notes, desire "so dominates a nature, that every fiber of the body, as every cell of the brain, seems to be instinct with fearful impulses. Men and women at such moments lose the freedom of their will. They move to their terrible end as automatons move" (191). If desire thus annuls the autonomy of the individual, this is finally because it undermines consciousness itself, making Dorian think in a circle in order to justify "passions that without such justification would still have dominated his temper" (187). Wilde's stress on the individual's loss of free will and of consciousness, on desire's ability to turn the individual into a thing, is subtly reinforced here by the implicit assumption that desire itself is the agent, dominating the individual, who becomes its object. This portrayal of desire would seem to re-present, as an internalized process, Wilde's sense of the ontological reversals implicit in the homoerotic, the notion that desire, based on the objectification of others, continually threatens to turn the self into an object to be desired by the other. It is hardly surprising that Dorian, dominated by passion, experiences an increasing sense of the "sickness" of his soul.

The terrors of desire, however, do not end with the danger of objectification. Finally, desire threatens the individual with the complete dissolution of the self. Desire, the novel suggests, can ultimately be characterized as a descent into the unstructured. Having embraced the new Hedonism, Dorian concludes that the "Ego in man" is not "simple, permanent, reliable, and of one essence" (146). Rather, "man" is a being "with myriad lives and myriad sensations, a complex multiform creature that bore within itself strange legacies of thought and passion" (146). Such legacies invoke contemporary notions of genetics that assumed the transmission of moral as well as physical characteristics (Russett

1989, 64–68). Contemplating the portraits of his ancestors, Dorian wonders what passions, what inheritance of "sin and shame" each has bequeathed. Reflecting on Philip Herbert, his ancestor during the reign of Queen Elizabeth, Dorian wonders whether it is "young Herbert's life that he sometimes led. Had some poisonous germ crept from body to body till it had reached his own?" (146). Such legacies are thus not merely multiple, a challenge to the notion of a coherent ego, but they also implicitly erase any firm distinction of self and other. Nor is the "legacy" confined to the genetic. One has "ancestors in literature" too, Dorian notes, who exert an "influence." As the use of the term *influence* suggests, these "strange figures" who have made sin "so marvelous" are not simply an external force but rather extensions of the self. To Dorian, it seems that "in some mysterious way their lives had been his own" (147), and the point is doubly reinforced by noting Dorian's identification with the hero of the "poisonous book," who himself attempts to reenact the lives of such historical figures as Tiberius and Caligula. If the "whole of history" comes to seem merely a record of Dorian's own life, then not only is the self dissolved into multiple identities, but the notion of any distinct ego separate from others ceases to exist.

Such legacies and influences are invariably linked to the "poisonous" in the novel and assimilated to a model of the transmission of disease, of the movement of "poisonous" germs. Not surprisingly, then, the desire for sensations itself moves from the quest for structured, aesthetic experiences to the pursuit of the chaotic, "the crude violence of disordered life" (187). It is therefore apt that desire comes to be associated in the novel with madness, a term that occurs with increasing frequency as the work progresses. This is not simply the "madness for pleasure" (154) that Dorian is said to communicate to his companions but finally pleasure as madness, as the dissolution of the self. Under the impact of desire, the self becomes a series of isolated moments of pleasure divorced from the past and from any larger coherence. Dorian's "mad craving" for opium is thus presented not simply as a desire for pleasure but precisely as the desire for discontinuity, to have the memory of "old sins" erased by "the madness of sins that were new" (186). Able not only to objectify the subject but to dissolve the self, as Dorian's experiences suggest, desire is finally presented as antithetical to identity.

Homosexual Desire in *The Picture of Dorian Gray*

If desire's effects recall the terrors of drug addiction and madness, it is hardly surprising that Wilde should refuse to embrace openly the full implications of Dorian's descent into desire. Even as he depicts the dangers of Dorian's pursuit of "sin," Wilde nonetheless attempts to conceal or minimize the effects of desire by subtly insisting on Dorian's status as a coherent and unified subject. This would seem, for example, to be the strategy underlying the novel's notorious chapter II, which depicts in copious detail Dorian's attempt to define a new spirituality by embracing sensory experience. Although, as we have seen, Dorian has constituted himself as an object, Wilde's focus on Dorian's exploration of the new Hedonism implicitly asserts Dorian's subjectivity by stressing his experience. Ultimately, however, this strategy serves as much to reveal as to conceal Dorian's objectification.

Although Dorian's stated goal is to blend "certain alien modes of thought" with sensory experience, the chapter in fact moves from Dorian's experiments with Catholicism and Darwinism to his sensuous appreciation of perfumes and music. Such a progression from cognition to sensation would have suggested a de-evolutionary movement to less complex forms of existence to a contemporary audience, and this movement is continued and extended by a shift of attention from Dorian's experience to his pursuit of material possessions. The chapter as a whole progresses from Dorian's sensory experiments to a discussion of his collections of jewels and fabrics, and a parallel progression is apparent in the sections detailing individual enthusiasms. Dorian's "flirtation" with Catholicism is reduced, finally, to a passion for collecting ecclesiastical vestments, and his sensory experience of music becomes an interest in collecting musical instruments. In short, Dorian is finally defined as a connoisseur rather than as an aesthete.

At first glance, this shift does not seem to challenge Dorian's status as a subject. Surely the role of the connoisseur, "the one who knows" the value of things, stresses the experiencing (and experienced) subject as fully as does the position of the aesthete, the individual sensitive to beauty. In fact, the two terms are generally taken to be synonymous. These roles, however, are based on a subtle but vital distinction. Unlike the aesthete, who focuses on the sensations produced by the beautiful, the connoisseur focuses on the beautiful object itself. Dorian's collections thus substitute possession of an object for experience, which cannot be possessed, and his search for the "spiritual mysteries" produced for him even by sensory experience is replaced by the commodity fetish:

> He longed to see the curious table napkins wrought for the Priest of the Sun, on which were displayed all the dainties and viands that could be wanted for a feast; the mortuary cloth of King Chilperic, with its three hundred golden bees; the fantastic robes that excited the indignation of the Bishop of Pontus, and were figured with "lions, panthers, bears, dogs, forests, rocks, hunters—all in fact that a painter can copy from nature"; and the coat that Charles of Orleans once wore, on the sleeves of which were embroidered the verses of a song beginning: *"Madame, je suis tout joyeux,"* the musical accompaniment of the words being wrought in gold thread, and each note, of square shape in those days, formed with four pearls. (141)

The list itself is telling. It seems hardly accidental that these cloths and robes objectify sensory experience—gustatory, visual, and auditory. In them, the world is reduced to representation, and they are thus isomorphic to Dorian's connoisseurship itself, in which possession of the material object is substituted for and represents the evanescence of sensory experience. Minimizing the sensory activity of the aesthete, the connoisseur would seem to retreat from subjectivity, and if these objects are finally cloth (coats, napkins, robes), such fabrics suggest the way in which pursuit of the commodity comes to veil any deeper perception. "These treasures and everything he had collected," we are told, serve finally as a "means of forgetfulness" (143) for Dorian. The implication here, however, is not simply that the quest for the commodity dulls subjectivity. As Walter Benjamin has pointed out, while the commodity fetish "couples the living body to the inorganic world," it simultaneously creates the illusion that the connoisseur, through his collections, is asserting his identity ([1955] 1986, 153–55). Even as it de-realizes the individual, the quest for objects conceals the collector's own status as an object. While Benjamin's analysis is intended to reveal the connoisseur as the type of the individual in a consumer society based on universal commodification, it takes on added resonance in the context of *Dorian Gray*. If the commodity fetish both conceals and confirms the individual's own reduction to an object, it is singularly apt that

Dorian should use it to deny his own objectification. Thus fabric finds its final use in the novel in the magnificent funeral pall that Dorian drapes across the portrait to conceal it, to hide "the living death of his own soul" (221), just as Dorian's collection of fabrics allows him to "forget" his wish to imitate the portrait's status as the object of desire. Ultimately, however, Dorian cannot completely forget, and Wilde's own attempt to confirm Dorian's status as a subject by insisting on his role as a connoisseur seems finally unsuccessful; the collector's submission to the "sex appeal of the inorganic" serves as much to recall as to deny the objectification associated with desire.[9]

A similar failure marks Wilde's attempts to recode the novel's presentation of the homoerotic erasure of the distinction of self and other by stressing Dorian's narcissism. Upon his first introduction to the narrative, Dorian is typologically identified by Lord Henry as Narcissus, a characterization that Dorian immediately confirms by falling in love with the portrait. The rest of the novel merely acts as a gloss upon this initial identification, expanding its complexity. Thus even after the portrait has begun to change, Dorian delights in sitting before it simply because the sharpness of the contrast to Dorian himself reinforces his awareness of his own beauty. Even more subtly, Dorian's narcissism leads him to be "more and more interested in the corruption of his own soul" (131), even his regret over his degeneration reflecting a pity that "was all the more poignant because it was purely selfish" (132). This "pride of individualism" (143) would seem to recuperate Dorian's status as a distinct entity, as a unified coherent ego. Portraying Dorian as ruthlessly egocentric, Wilde is able not only to mystify the disintegrative effects of desire on the personality but also to explain Dorian's transmutation into an object by attributing it to an intense self-fascination. The reification of the self is thus seen as the result of too much self-coherence rather than too little, as an excess of individuality rather than as its absence.[10]

The central device that animates the narrative, however—the division of Dorian into a physical body and a psychic entity, the portrait—immediately undermines this strategy. To begin with, this split problematizes the notion of a monadic self. If the portrait is said to contain Dorian's "soul," then the traditional assumption of the self as unified is called into question, and the reader is forced to reexamine the Narcissus story. Instead of the individual closed in upon himself, Narcissus can be seen to represent the impossibility of the self, the continual interplay of self and other. The epitome of Lacan's mirror stage, Narcissus sees reflected in the water a self that is in fact the other, outside the self. As such, Narcissus becomes an emblem of the fluidity of self and other, of the individual and the world.

The problem is not merely that the self is also the other, that the portrait, the external object, is said to be Dorian's "self." As Julian Hawthorne has noted, the "portrait is rather the more real thing of the two" ([1890] 1970, 80), and the painting takes on the status of subject in the scopic economy, while Dorian becomes the object displayed to incite the desire of the other. Thus Dorian calls in the frame maker to carry the portrait to the attic room so that his "soul" will be hidden "from the eyes of men" (125), and as the frame maker and his assistant descend the stairs, the assistant glances back at Dorian with a look of "shy wonder," since he has "never seen anyone so marvelous" (127). In fact, the relations between Dorian and his portrait themselves reenact the continual reversibility of subject and object found in male relations in the novel. While Dorian may look at the portrait, it is frequently the portrait who watches Dorian, "looking out at him from the canvas" (123). Basil calls attention to this fact when he is finally shown the altered picture. It is, he notes, leering at them, and the subject status of the painting is confirmed when Dorian is filled with a feeling of hatred for Basil that seems to have been suggested by the portrait, "whispered into his ear by those grinning lips" (160). Wilde's attempts to insist on the possibility of a unified subject, distinct from the external world and immune to the perils of objectification, thus fail, and these failures are summarized in the central symbol of the novel. The portrait not only problematizes the ideal of the coherent self, undercutting even the Narcissus legend upon which the ideal is based, but also underlines the tenuousness of the roles of subject and object.

ENACTING INCOHERENCE

Unlike earlier Victorian fiction, in which the dangers associated with sexuality are successfully contained by various strategies,

Wilde's techniques for restraining the anarchic potential of homosexuality thus prove inadequate. Instead, the incoherence attributed to the homoerotic desire that provides the novel's content affects the work itself so that the novel not only represents but enacts that incoherence. This is nowhere more apparent than in the moral contradictions of the text. As Lord Henry notes, "Nothing is ever quite true" (84); and critics have often pointed out that the work is torn between an affirmation of the principles of the new Hedonism and a conventional moral affirming the necessity of punishment for sin. By the same token, even the most minimal principles of logical coherence sometimes seem to be suspended in the novel. Thus Basil can affirm that every portrait is really a portrait of the artist and, within a few pages, assert that "an artist should create beautiful things, but should put nothing of his own life into them" (19). Like Dorian himself, the novel dissolves into a series of discontinuous moments.[11]

Moreover, the work's subject matter seems to promote a curious dislocation in the language of the novel, which enacts the polymorphous attractions of the homoerotic by multiplying "metaphors as monstrous as orchids" (129). Drawing together the most disparate realms, the general thrust of the novel's language is to reduce the animate to the inanimate ("like a blue thread a long, thin dragonfly floated past on its brown gauze wings" [14]) or the human to the nonhuman. Thus the Duchess of Monmouth's teeth show "like white seeds in a scarlet fruit" (207), and James Vane's face is pressed against the conservatory window "like a white handkerchief" (200). Such comparisons confirm Wilde's presentation of the effects of desire by reducing subjects to objects, but they also extend the "in-difference" associated with (homo)sexuality by eradicating conventional "logical" distinctions. Unlike the metaphysical conceit, in which the startling conjunction of disparate objects is intended to disclose the hidden order of the universe, the metaphors in *Dorian Gray* seem to unveil the tenuousness of the cultural taxonomies imposed upon existence. It is thus apt that the metaphors themselves repeatedly call attention to the monstrous. From the parasols that dip and dance "like monstrous butterflies" to the sky that appears like a "monstrous peacock's tail," the novel's metaphors suggest a universe beyond conventional logic in which the ultimate monstrosity is the erasure of difference, of logical distinction itself. The language of the novel is thus finally "homosexual" in the sense that it proliferates polymorphous connections, dislocating the familiar linguistic and conceptual map placed upon the world.

Wilde is writing during a period in which that map was being called into question, an era of what Elaine Showalter, following Gissing, has called "sexual anarchy." Showalter invokes the term to discuss the collapse of previous certainties, specifically the contemporary crisis of ideas of gender, but it also refers to the problematization of (hetero)sexuality and, with Freud, of the nature of the subject and of identity (1990, 1–14). In such a context, Wilde seems unable to frame his discussion of the sexual. The problem is compounded by contemporary definitions of homosexuality itself as the locus of the dangers associated with the sexual. Seen as "in-different" and anarchic, polymorphous and chaotic, articulated as the Other of heterosexuality, homosexuality is ideologically positioned outside of the very possibilities of "structure" and "logic" themselves. As such, the novel cannot contain the chaotic effects associated with homosexual desire but can only reproduce or enact them by becoming logically and linguistically "incoherent."

Precisely because the chaos associated with the sexual is crystallized in the notion of homosexuality, Wilde's text not only summarizes the sexual fears of the Victorian novel but also uncovers an anxiety latent in earlier representations of sex and sexuality. Wilde's novel illustrates the concerns we have seen in Austen, Gaskell, and Dickens: that the sexual challenges the very principles of binarism and taxonomy that ground Victorian conceptualizations of the world, that it can erase or disrupt particular binary oppositions and familiar taxonomies, ranging from the class structure and the gender system to the distinctions of self and other or subject and object. Ultimately, however, Wilde's novel uncovers an even deeper fear: an anxiety not about difference but about meaning, about the possibility of representation itself. Dissolving into incoherence, the text suggests that sex and sexuality can disrupt the novel itself, that the resistance of the sexual to representation, its tendency to disrupt attempts to represent it, will shatter the very form intended to define and contain it. Just as the idea of homosexuality summarizes Victorian notions of the sexual as anarchic, the collapse of Wilde's text reveals Victorian fears that sexuality will destroy the structures not only of Victorian culture but of Victorian fiction.

As Showalter notes, the fin-de-siècle is also a period of textual anarchy, of changing notions of the nature and structure of the novel (1990, 15–18). Precisely because Wilde's novel cannot contain the anarchic desire it portrays, Wilde's text implicitly revises some of the basic assumptions that ground Victorian fiction. As I suggested in chapter 2, the Victorian novel is constituted by a sense of interiority, of hidden forces and meanings and of a truth that cannot be directly spoken. This truth, based on an analogy between the novel and the subjectivity of the individual, is always linked in some way to the sexual in Victorian fiction, the hidden secret at the core of the nineteenth-century novel. Wilde cannot entirely escape this belief that the novel has an interiority, a belief that persists into our own day, yet the continual stress in *Dorian Gray* on desire's ability to turn the subject into an object seems finally to affect Wilde's construction of the novel and to create new assumptions about fiction and sexual representation. As Jonathan Dollimore has argued, Wilde's sense that "transgressive desire" calls into question the depth model of subjectivity led to an aesthetic philosophy that emphasized the surface of the work of art (1991, 3–18). Rejecting the idea of a narrative interior, of a "secret" at the novel's core, Wilde thus inverts the "narrative repression" initiated by Austen and foreshadows a radically different conception of both the novel and the representation of sex and sexuality.

Certainly, the notion of hidden depths in *Dorian Gray* is problematic as far as the characters are concerned. Having murdered Basil, Dorian attends a party at Lady Narborough's where he is amazed at his ability to "play a part" and at the calm of his demeanor, and he feels keenly "the terrible pleasure of a double life" (177). At first glance, this would seem to be the imaginative crux of the novel, the contrast between Dorian's innocent appearance and the corruption of his soul, between the charming dandy kissing his hostess's hand and the portrait hidden in the locked room. The central assumptions of the novel, however, are precisely the opposite: that nothing is ever really hidden. On the most basic level, secrets do not exist in the work. Certainly there is constant reference to the secrets of the characters: to Sibyl's secret (her love for Dorian), to Mrs. Vane's secret (the illegitimacy of her children), to Basil's secret (his idolatry of Dorian). Yet such secrets are no sooner presented than they are disclosed: Sibyl confesses to her mother, Mrs. Vane to her son, Basil to Lord Henry and, eventually, to Dorian himself. In fact, they must, not so much to animate the plot as to conform to Wilde's assumptions, for the premise of the work is that there are no hidden depths, that everything is evident on the surface.

Apparently predicated on Dorian's secret, the work is based, in reality, on the portrait's visual presentation of Dorian's sins, on the conceit that all of Dorian's vices and emotions are evident in the portrait, which is the "visible symbol" of the degradation of sin (100). The wicked are always old and ugly, notes Hetty, the innocent country girl whom Dorian decides not to seduce, but the same view is presented at length by Basil: "Sin is a thing that writes itself across a man's face. It cannot be concealed. People talk sometimes of secret vices. There are no such things. If a wretched man has a vice, it shows itself in the lines of his mouth, the droop of his eyelids, the moulding of his hands, even" (152). In both contexts, the assumption is that Dorian must be good because he is beautiful, and the novel plays on the ironic disjunction of Dorian's beauty and the corruption of his soul, but the premise underlying the progressive disintegration of the portrait is in fact the same: that sin and corruption are indeed visibly apparent. The contrast between appearance and reality, surface and depth, that animates so much of Victorian fiction is displaced here into the contrast of two surfaces, the appearances of Dorian and of his portrait. The most telling phrase in the work may in fact be that the portrait "held the secret of his life, and told his story" (96). Evident on the surface, the secret of sin must always be told.

This refusal of depths and secrets is paralleled by the aesthetic philosophy presented in the work. Although art is seen in the novel as the reflection of something higher, and Basil's art, Lord Henry concludes, is implicitly Neoplatonic, it still requires Dorian as its "visible emblem," as the "visible incarnation of that unseen ideal" (118). In and of itself, this perspective need not deny the higher reality that the visible embodies, yet the ideal seems curiously unattainable in the novel, the emphasis falling rather on the visible incarnation. Thus, although Dorian becomes the ideal of the young men of his age, a combination of the culture of the scholar and the manner of a "citizen of the world," this ideal itself is reduced to the "worship of beauty," to an emphasis on the visible appearance rather than the unseen ideal. As the narrator notes, quoting Gautier, Dorian is one for whom "the visible world existed" (132). The prospect of an art in which the beautiful surface is valued more than any hidden meaning is further confirmed by Wilde's equation of art and society. Noting that the canons of good society are the same as those of art, the narrator elucidates, stressing that both require the "dignity of a ceremony" and that form is "absolutely essential" to both. In art as well as society, then, the emphasis falls on the surface rather than on content, an emphasis that characterizes literature as well. As the maxims that preface *Dorian Gray* note: "All art is at once surface and symbol. Those who go beneath the surface do so at their peril. Those who read the symbol do so at their peril."[12]

It is hardly surprising, then, that Gide, speaking of the novel's style, noted Wilde's tendency to a "prodigious overloading of concetti," with the "result that the glittering of the surface makes our mind lose sight of the deep central emotion" ([1949] 1969, 34n). The more closely the reader looks at the novel, however, the more problematic becomes the notion that there is any deep central emotion in the work at all. Wilde's goal would seem to be, finally, to reject meaning and to turn the text into an object, to empty it of its interiority. This construction of the text not only parallels the objectification of the characters but extrapolates the implications of such objectification. If the work's portrayal of homosexual desire calls into question the possibility of the self, of the subject, then the subjectivity of the text, predicated on our notions of the self, must be equally suspect. Overwhelmed by the "de-repressed" desire that forms its subject matter, *Dorian Gray* becomes a "de-repressed narrative," a story without any secrets, sexual or otherwise. Problematizing the notion of the interiority of the novel, *Dorian Gray* challenges a basic assumption underlying Victorian fiction and brings Wilde to the verge of modernism, to a focus on form rather than content.

Surely it is homosexuality itself that is *the* secret of the novel, the sexual secret—the secret of the sexual—that both must and cannot be spoken. Is not Wilde's novel finally yet another example of the Victorian notion that any love can only speak its name indirectly? Certainly, recent examinations of Wilde's work have interpreted it, often brilliantly, as an attempt precisely to represent, in a coded form, the "unspeakable" sin. Thus Christopher Craft reads *The Importance of Being Earnest* as a critique of heterosexual representation that articulates homosexual desire in the vertiginous, polysemic possibilities of language itself (1990, 19–46), and Ed Cohen argues that the characters in *Dorian Gray* must seek discursive options for a sexuality that cannot be represented in the language of the dominant culture (1987, 806). Similarly, Eve Sedgwick sees homosexuality as covertly figured in the novel's play of sentimental and antisentimental currents (1990, 131–81). Such analyses would seem to clarify why, despite its relentless disclosures, there is one secret that the novel does keep. Although *Dorian Gray* openly presents murder and drug addiction and notes in passing the fallen women ruined by Dorian, ultimately the narrator refuses to disclose the "hideous things" that are whispered about Dorian. These "things," the unstated vices that make his friendship so "fatal to young men," have usually been glossed as homosexual relations, the final repository of Victorian notions of the anarchic potential and ineffability of the sexual. I would argue, however, that (homo)sexuality does not provide the interior of the text. The point is not simply that the novel fooled no one, that it presented, as Eve Sedgwick has suggested, an "open secret" (1990, 164).[13] Nor is it simply that, by enacting Wilde's sense of the homoerotic, the novel itself, like Dorian's portrait, openly displays homosexuality on its surface in the disintegration and objectification of the text. Finally, Wilde's novel is both more radical and more modern than the novels that precede it. For Wilde finally calls into question the entire nineteenth-century enterprise of representing the sexual, interrogating the very assumptions underlying the Victorian novel's technologies of erotic representation.

As we have seen, the representation of sex and sexuality in the Victorian novel is based on a sense that the sexual is chaotic in its effects and in its nature. As I have suggested, such representation serves less to repress sex and sexuality than to produce them, if only by defining them as chaotic. Thus, if sex and sexuality are "repressed" in Victorian fiction, this is not because they are not directly spoken. Rather, it is because they are represented, however indirectly or mediately. If the sexual is, finally, the "real"—

that extralinguistic reality that always exceeds any attempt to represent it—then the actual repression of sex and sexuality is its representation, not just in language, but in narrative, with its rules of coherence and its assumption of expressibility, of a "meaning" to the story. Finally, narrative represses the sexual not because it hides it but because it speaks it, suggesting that it can be articulated and bounded, taking its place in the hierarchical structures of the meaning of the text. Thwarted or gratified, the sexual desires of the characters in narrative are made clear and concluded. For author and readers, the narrative suggests that the sex and sexuality it speaks can have a meaning and can be made compatible with the narrative order and the order of narrative.

However dimly or unconsciously, Wilde seems to be aware of this principle. If *The Picture of Dorian Gray* details the thrilling and terrifying effects on the characters of a "de-repressed" desire, a desire that exceeds the cultural restraints of Oedipal heterosexuality, it does so in a narrative that is itself thrilling and terrifying in another fashion. To read the novel's secret as "homosexuality" is finally to underestimate the implications of Wilde's narrative. Wilde's refusal of closure, his denial of a final answer, does not merely suggest that homoerotic desire cannot be directly articulated in a homophobic culture or that all sexuality is finally unspeakable in the sense that it is chaotically unavailable to any narrativization. Finally, in typically paradoxical fashion, Wilde reverses the ideological grounding of the representation of the sexual in the Victorian novel, the sense that sex and sexuality cannot be spoken but that they must nonetheless enter discourse. Rather, Wilde suggests, the sexual can be spoken (indeed, as we have seen, the Victorian novel always produces or enacts it), but it *should not* be articulated. Breaking the rules of stories, which provide narrative closure by explaining everything, Wilde thus leaves one mystery, implying that sexuality has no clear meaning, no answer. Just as *Dorian Gray* anticipates modernism in its attention to the (formal) surface of the work at the expense of an (interior) content, so Wilde's novel thus adumbrates the contradictions of a twentieth-century attitude toward the sexual, which realizes that the freedom to discuss the erotic is itself a repression, that any articulation of sex and sexuality falsely constructs a fixed "meaning" for them. Ultimately, Wilde rejects this repression in a refusal of representation that both ends the Victorian novel and inaugurates the modern era. Asked to clarify the nature of Dorian's vices, Wilde declined: "Each man sees his own sin in Dorian Gray. What Dorian's sins are no one knows. He who finds them has brought them" (1979, 82). Like the imperfect pleasures of sex and sexuality that it invokes but refuses to name, *The Picture of Dorian Gray* is both exquisite and leaves the reader unsatisfied, the perfect type of a new conception of the sexual and of new (im)possibilities of representation.

Notes

Chapter 1

1. Research in the past thirty years has produced varied assessments of Victorian sexual attitudes and of their impact on Victorian fiction. Houghton (1957, 353–58) and Stone (1977, 673–77) present the traditional picture of the era as almost impossibly prudish. Goldfarb (1970) argues that, as a result, sexuality is largely hidden or unconscious in the literature of the period. As a counterbalance to this perspective, Marcus ([1966] 1985) and Pearsall (1969) portray the Victorians as the creators and consumers of a vast underworld of sexual pleasures, both in pornographic literature and in life. Recently a moderate position has emerged that reconciles these emphases. Gay (1984) argues that despite a policy of calculated ignorance on these matters, the Victorians demonstrate a far greater experience of and familiarity with sensuality than subsequent generations have sometimes been willing to allow them. Erotic enjoyment was offset by sexual anxiety, however. Relegated to private life, sexuality was circumscribed by discretion, public reticence, and observance of sexually restrictive social convention. See also Johnson 1975 (16–21) and Weeks 1981 (19–23). Victorian literature, although necessarily discreet by virtue of its public status, displays a similar balance between attempts to deal frankly with life and self-censorship on the subject of sex (Gay 1986, 197). Trudgill (1976, 155–247) charts the often subtle shifts in the relative strength of prudish and sensual currents in English culture from 1750 to 1900.

2. For discussions linking sexual reticence in the Victorian novel to the Evangelical movement, see Houghton 1957 (359), Goldfarb 1970 (22), Johnson 1975 (20), and Weeks 1981 (27).

3. Note, however, that Heath inverts the relation of the two terms as articulated by Foucault, subsuming *sex* under *sexuality*.

4. As Deirdre David (n.d.) has demonstrated, these perceptions are equally apparent in British reactions to India, particularly in Anglo-Indian attempts to eradicate thuggee cults.

5. For an analysis of nineteenth-century associations between blacks, the sexualized woman, and disease, see Gilman 1985 (76–108). It is worth noting that, like the snake it conceals, the gold in Africa's lap is an implicitly phallic image, given Victorian conceptions of male sexual activity as analogous to economic expenditure. For the latter idea, see Heath 1984 (14–18).

6. An alternate Victorian strategy for maintaining the class system, as Catherine Gallagher's analysis of Malthus and Mayhew suggests, is to deny biological universality by insisting on a taxonomy of bodies, on the existence of innate corporeal differences between the members of various social and economic groups (1987, 90–91). In effect, Darwin employs a similar tactic. If *The Origin* confirms and contributes to Victorian perceptions of nature as chaotic, Darwin's retreat from this vision is to insist implicitly that nature is in fact "ordered." Darwin effects this construction less through his insistence on the validity of taxonomy (since "taxonomy" is now suspended between the earlier idea that biological classification inheres in nature and an emerging sense that it is a convenient fiction) than through the more modern idea that the natural world is ordered, not by transcendental classifications, but by "laws" such as descent with modification.

7. Clearly, then, the "Victorian" perceptions I have been discussing must be recognized as a hegemonic perspective serving the interests of the bourgeois white male. The most extensively analyzed aspect of this ideology is its constitution of the feminine. In this context, Mary Poovey's analysis (1988) of the Victorians' binary construction of gender, and the use of this construction as the difference that grounded, and occluded, differences of class, race, and national identity, is particularly helpful (see especially 3–15 and 75–80). See also Laqueur 1990 (193–243), Birken 1988 (72–91), Armstrong 1987 (161–86), and Russett 1989 (1–15, 192–206). I will discuss nineteenth-century constructions of gender difference in chapter 3. For analyses of the function of binarism in the creation of both gender and racial stereotypes, see Gilman 1985 (15–35) and Sinha 1987. Brantlinger analyzes the intersection of constructions of racial and class alterity (1988, 183–84).

8. The problem is not unique to Victorian literature. Even such eras as the eighteenth and twentieth centuries, which impose fewer restrictions on sexual frankness in literature, encounter the failure of language to articulate the essence of sexual experience. This is perhaps especially evident in pornography, which, attempting to move closer to an expression of the sexual, ends up further away, its language ossifying into clichés and formulaic descriptions. It is this very deadness of the language, Marcus notes, that suggests that sexual experience, the "meaning" of pornography, is "beyond language" ([1966] 1985, 240).

9. Given its potential to ignore differences in social class and background, love would also seem to pose a threat to the social structure. As Joseph Allen Boone has noted, however, the ideal of romantic love leading to marriage not only provides much of the subject matter of most Victorian novels but even shapes their narrative structure (1987, 71–80). If love fails to generate fears of social instability and an anxious reticence in Victorian fiction, the reason would seem to lie in the nature of its construction by Western culture. While sex, for the Victorians, is grounded, however ineffably, in biology, in a natural realm per-

ceived as antithetical to culture, love is associated with the same ideas as society itself. Largely invented by the troubadours of the twelfth century, as de Rougemont ([1956] 1974) and Stone (1977, 282–87) have made clear, the ideology of love is taxonomic and hierarchical, predicated on a belief in the uniqueness and ontological superiority of the love object (as the long tradition in romantic comedy of the secret nobility of the foundling suggests). If sex is perceived as intrinsically "democratic," based on a universal human sameness, love is "aristocratic," grounded on the principle of difference. Thus, as Robert Polhemus has convincingly argued, the nineteenth-century novel replaces religious conviction with "erotic faith," the belief that transcendence can be found through love (1990, 1–27). For a complete discussion of Victorian views of love, see Gay 1986. Although the Victorian novel focuses on love, relegating sex to the subtext, in practice the two are not so easily separated; as Gay notes, the common Victorian ideal of romantic love is a mixture of affection and eroticism that subsumes the sexual (1986, 44–95).

Chapter 2

1. Modern critics who argue that Austen openly portrays sexuality often invert this process, subsuming the romantic under the sexual. See, for example, Fergus 1981 (66–85), McMaster 1978 (67–75), and Smith 1983 (96–100). Austen's indirect presentation of sexuality through literary allusions, puns, and sexual symbols has been discussed by Chandler (1975, 88–103).

2. Although my use of the words *homosexual* and *heterosexual* here is somewhat anachronistic, since the terms were not invented until the end of the nineteenth century, a concept of homosexual desire as same-sex object choice had begun to emerge at the end of the eighteenth century (Bray 1982, 81–114). Thus a similar association of transvestism not only with the erasure of gender difference but also with homosexuality was a feature of eighteenth-century antimasquerade literature (Castle 1986, 46–47). In chapter 5 I provide a detailed discussion of the emergence of a fully developed notion of homosexuality at the end of the nineteenth century, and of the resulting realignment of Victorian conceptions of the sexual field.

3. Chapman, in his "Index of Characters," lists Chamberlayne as a member of the militia (Austen [1813] 1932, 413). The sole reference to him in the novel is the passage cited, however, and his identity is not very clear. It is conceivable that he is a servant, which would suggest the additional possibility of a violation of class distinctions. It is also worth noting that sexual desire indirectly calls gender difference into question here. If, as Armstrong (1987, 41) suggests, part of the contemporary definition of the genders is based on the idea of a "natural" attraction to the opposite sex, then the possibility of same-sex desire elides one of the distinctions between "men" and "women." Although the gender boundaries erased by Chamberlayne's cross-dressing are almost immediately restored by the disclosure of the joke, the problematization of contemporary ideas of gender difference by the polymorphous potential of sexual desire—in this case the possibility of homosexual attraction—cannot be so easily recuperated.

4. Austen's attitude toward her society has been the subject of extensive debate. Claudia Johnson (1988, 73–93), Sandra Gilbert and Susan Gubar (1979, 146–83), and Marvin Mudrick (1952) have argued that Austen is covertly opposed to contemporary social values. I agree with Marilyn Butler (1975, 197–218), Alistair Duckworth (1971, 5–10), and Deborah Kaplan (1992, 182–205) that Austen is essentially a conservative novelist, concerned with the maintenance of orthodox values and the existing social structure. Note that the apparent class mobility represented by Elizabeth's marriage to Darcy is relatively minor. She is a gentleman's daughter, as she insists to Lady Catherine, and not another Pamela.

5. Austen's model here, of course, is not Lacan but Samuel Johnson. The impossibility of perfect happiness and the eternal renewal of desire is the theme, for example, of *Rasselas,* where the quest for satisfaction is also represented by the metaphor of the journey. For a discussion of Johnson's association of desire with disorder, see Patricia Meyer Spacks 1990 (18–21). Compare Claudia Johnson's assertion that Austen follows Dr. Johnson in insisting that the pursuit of happiness is "the business of life" (1988, 77–81).

6. As Mary Poovey notes, this structure not only is moral but also works imaginatively to resolve an ideological contradiction in Austen's society, namely, the conflict between an increasing bourgeois stress on the needs of the individual and an older emphasis on the stability of an authoritarian social system. On the level of plot, the mortification of Elizabeth's pride suggests that egotism must be restrained, reconciled with the social structure. By rewarding Elizabeth with Darcy, however, Austen is also able to suggest to the reader that the wishes of the individual will be fulfilled (1984, 194–207).

7. As Regenia Gagnier makes clear, this notion of the subject as an autonomous, individualized self-consciousness is a bourgeois construction that should not be equated with eighteenth- and nineteenth-century working-class subjectivity, which was predicated on communal experience (1991, 31–54, 141–49).

8. As Darcy's behavior in *Pride and Prejudice* demonstrates, the ideal of sexual self-regulation was extended to men during the nineteenth century (Gay 1984, 58). However, the doctrine was applied to women not only earlier but more stringently, as the eighteenth-century notion of woman as an inherently sexual being whose desires must be (self-)regulated was replaced by the nineteenth-century implantation of sexual restraint in women as an intrinsic, "natural" attribute of the gender (Poovey 1988, 9–10). Certainly, the latter conception allows individual women fewer behavioral choices and less latitude for self-definition. In a sense, Austen's novel illustrates this ideological shift. Rather than dramatizing an internal struggle between feminine sexuality and self-restraint, Austen projects the conflict outward, juxtaposing such self-regulated characters as Elizabeth and Jane to the passionate Lydia. While such a technique acknowledges female sexuality, it also paves the way for the Victorian notion of women as inherently passionless by presenting repression *or* passion as the "nature" of individuals. As such, the abjection of Lydia from the narrative both foreshadows and enacts the excision of sexuality from the Victorian construction of woman. For a slightly different reading of the gendering of sexual self-restraint in relation to contemporary ideas of love, see Polhemus 1990 (50–52).

9. The sexual implications of dancing, one of the major tropes in Austen's

fiction, have been extensively discussed. See Adams 1982 (55–65), Elsbree 1960 (113–36), Smith 1983 (88), Mansell 1973 (8–9), Polhemus 1990 (41–42), and Sulloway 1989 (138–59). For discussions of Austen's use of vision to indicate sexual attraction and walking as a metaphor for sexual relationships, see, respectively, Willis 1976 (156–62) and Chandler 1975 (88–103).

10. Although the semiotics of sexual feeling may be unclear, as when Darcy is unable to discern Jane's interest in Bingley early in the novel, such signs are not usually false. As Poovey notes, the contemporary idea of the "speaking countenance" assumes an unproblematic link between internal states of emotion and corporeal signs (1984, 24). Once again, this principle applies not only to the female but to the male characters in the novel. Thus the Gardiners are able, by observing him at Lambton, to determine Darcy's attraction to Elizabeth.

Chapter 3

1. As Thomas Laqueur has demonstrated, the notion of gender as a binary opposition based on biologically distinct male and female bodies is a relatively recent invention. Prior to the eighteenth century, Laqueur argues, the "sexes" were construed according to a hierarchical "one sex" model that perceived male and female as different in degree rather than in kind. Moreover, Laqueur notes, post-Enlightenment notions of biology or the body as the epistemic foundation for the cultural meanings of gender invert an earlier idea of gender as the transcendental "reality" and of the body as its epiphenomenon (1990, 1–24).

2. To a lesser extent, death is also used in the novel to represent the threat posed by nature to culture. Because death inescapably asserts the existence of the body and because it is "common," further evidence of biological universality and the artificiality of class distinctions, awareness of death must be repressed. Thus it is "a word not to be mentioned to ears polite" (4). The inevitability of death, however, implied by its recurrent use in *Cranford*'s plot, again suggests the unavoidable return of repressed biology.

3. Such an insistence on class difference does not preclude—in fact, it could be said to make possible—the sympathy for, and the desire to educate and "elevate," the working classes evident in Gaskell's social problem novels: *North and South* and *Mary Barton*. Precisely because the classes are seen as intrinsically different and hierarchically ordered, concern with working-class welfare becomes a moral duty for the middle classes.

4. By the same token, it seems hardly accidental that the vast majority of the novel's male characters are in some branch of military service. From Signor Brunoni, a former sergeant, to Peter, who becomes a lieutenant, from Major Gordon to Captain Brown, the men who come to Cranford are military men. The insistent association of men and the military seems designed to ground gender by linking the male characters to an immutably masculine preserve.

5. This conception of the implications of motherhood is not limited to the Victorian period. Thus, in *The Reproduction of Mothering*, Nancy Chodorow asserts that women lack a sense of distinction between self and other: "The basic feminine sense of self is connected to the world, the basic masculine sense of self

is separate" (1978, 169). Chodorow argues that this identification derives from a woman's psychological experience of her own mother during infancy. Inflecting the Victorian doctrine through object-relations psychology, Chodorow argues that same-sex children (daughters) retain their pre-Oedipal identification with the mother, while opposite-sex children (sons) do not. The result is a distinction in female and male conceptions of self, which are carried into adult life. Because of their "retention of preoedipal attachments to their mother, growing girls come to define and experience themselves as continuous with others; their experience of self contains more flexible or permeable ego boundaries. Boys come to define themselves as more separate and distinct, with a greater sense of rigid ego boundaries and differentiation" (169).

6. As Rowena Fowler points out (1984, 719–21), Gaskell also distinguishes gender by making a distinction between men's language and women's language in the novel, contrasting the "hard-edged public speech" of the male characters with the "lateral logic" and association of ideas that characterize the language of Cranford's women. Joseph Allen Boone convincingly argues that these characteristics of women's language are also reproduced in the novel's "centric structure," its rejection of (male) linear plotting in favor of an episodic organization based on incremental repetition and narrative circularity (1987, 295–304). The definitive reading of gendered language in Victorian women's writing is Margaret Homans's analysis of the distinction between (male) figurative language and (female) literal language (1986, 153–77, 223–76). For a historicized analysis of *Cranford* as an "experiment with narrative" that critiques and rewrites the masculine tradition of the Victorian novel, see Schor 1989 (288–304).

7. The equation of women and gardens and the related symbolization of woman as flower were clichés in contemporary art and literature (Dijkstra 1986, 14–17). It is thus appropriate that Peter's transvestite imitation of Deborah should take place in the garden and involve some initial confusion over whether the crowd is looking at Peter or a flower. The ultimate scandal of Peter's masquerade, then, may be not only that he penetrates a feminine space but also that he adopts, and thus "violates," the metaphors of femininity.

8. The representations generated here are male ideas of gender difference. If Gaskell accedes to them, however, their status as ideas also allows her to manipulate them. Thus Gaskell creates her definition of woman through the selection of a relatively positive reading of female physiology—as the source of the "maternal instinct"—in contrast to alternate, contemporary constructions of it as pathological, of woman as, inherently, disease and disorder. For discussions of the latter concept, see Poovey 1988 (37) and Russett 1989 (30–31, 116–19).

9. This technique also resolves the contradictory implications of Gaskell's own use of the maternal ideal. Implicitly based on a universal female body, this ideal suggests a similarity among women that conflicts with Gaskell's belief in class difference. Divorced from the body and transformed into woman's "nature," into a psychological state (selflessness) and a set of social relations (the blurring of self and other), the maternal ideal can be reconciled to Gaskell's insistence on (class) difference; the feminine becomes susceptible to individual variations and different class inflections, and is made compatible with both the Cranford ladies' sexual repression and Martha's sexual activity.

Chapter 4

1. In contrast, the mortality rate is approximately 7 percent in *Martin Chuzzlewit* and 11 percent in *Our Mutual Friend.*

2. This doubtless reflects Dickens's own uncertainty about the possibility of an afterlife. See Welsh 1971 (196) and Hutter 1983 (1–39).

3. Compare Sadoff 1982, in which the author argues that the discovery of origin and identity in *Bleak House,* as in much of Dickens's fiction, involves a quest for the father as the source of both the individual and of the events generating the narrative. The originary role of the father in Dickens is simultaneously suggested and concealed, Sadoff argues, because of Dickens's confrontation with the "primal scene" of his own engendering: his desire both to come to terms with the father as his own (sinful) origin and the desire not to know (11–22). For an alternative reading of Dickens's novels as the recurrent figuring of an authorial "primal scene," in this case his employment at Warren's Blacking Warehouse, see Lukacher 1986 (290–330).

4. For an analysis of the moral dimension of Lady Dedlock's lapse, see Blain 1985 (31–46). Blain reads the novel as a complex process of scapegoating in which male sexual appetite can be indulged and simultaneously denied through the repudiation of female sexuality, personified by Lady Dedlock, whose death purges transgressions against sexual purity. While Blain's argument correctly reflects the moral stress on female purity in Victorian culture as a whole, the fate of Nemo, who also dies a social outcast, suggests that Dickens is not simply concerned to reinforce conventional standards of feminine sexual conduct in *Bleak House.*

5. Compare D. A. Miller's assertion that Dickens is concerned with sexual transgressions against the social order in the novel (1988, 72). See also Philip Weinstein's argument that Dickens sympathizes with desire but fears the irrational passions that threaten the "altruistic norms of identity" that stabilize society in Dickens's novels (1984, 70).

6. Originally noted by Alex Zwerdling (1973, 429–39), the point has been made most recently by Christine van Boheeman, who stresses the implicit sexual implications of the "pox" Esther contracts (1987, 119). Compare Helena Michie's argument that illness in Dickens, rather than fragmenting identity, allows women the possibility of a discourse with which to articulate the body and the self (1989, 199–212).

7. If Dickens attempts to articulate death but not the sexual, this is perhaps because, ironically, literal death is less threatening to identity than the "deaths" induced by sexuality. As Stewart notes (1984, 14–17), physical death in literature actually serves to reinforce a character's identity because his or her nature is summed up in the metaphors used to trope that death. See also Miller 1988 (91). This does not prevent Dickens from using the idea of death to indicate the loss of identity induced by sexuality.

8. The cases of Krook and Richard also suggest that strong emotions of any sort can induce not only literal death but radical changes in identity. Thus Richard, "worn away" by his intense involvement in the Chancery suit, reverts to his youthful self on his deathbed. For his part, Krook literally dissolves.

9. For a radically different perspective on sexuality, desire, and repression in Dickens, see Kucich 1987 (201–83).

10. The major exception to this principle is Mr. George, whose body is described in some detail and presented less as an index of personality than as evidence of George's former occupation as a soldier. The description also notes George's "broad chest" and "sinewy" hands (305–6). Like this stress on George's physical power, the corporeal description itself associates George with the potentially violent emotions of the "vicious body," making him a credible suspect when Tulkinghorn is murdered.

11. See, for example, Frank 1984 (107) for the former point and Kucich 1981 (147) for the latter. Cynthia Malone reads the veiled figure in the novel as evidence that the self in *Bleak House* is always anonymous and multiple (1990, 107–24).

12. For a comprehensive analysis of the problems of representation in Dickens, see Kincaid 1987 (95–111).

13. The complexity of Freud's text and its implications for our understanding of nineteenth-century conceptions of sexuality (and of gender) can only be adumbrated here. For a more complete discussion of *Dora,* see Jacobus 1986 (137–93), Gallop 1982 (132–50), Rose 1986 (27–47), Sprengnether 1985 (51–71), and the essays collected in Bernheimer and Kahane 1985.

14. Stewart (1978, 457) notes that the phrase suggests Hawdon's relation to Esther as well as an ironic retribution for his guilt.

15. As we shall see, *Bleak House* is a text of pleasure rather than a text of bliss, for the novel centers precisely around a rejection of *jouissance.* For the distinction, see Barthes 1975 (14).

16. As D. A. Miller has brilliantly illustrated (1988, 69–73), the novel's use of the detective plot and of the figure of the detective also reflects a desire for the simplification and limitation of the totalizing social and institutional mechanisms of power represented in the novel by Chancery. As Miller notes, however, both the detective and his plot finally serve to reproduce those mechanisms.

17. Mrs. Snagsby's detective efforts do, however, reflect the inverted power relation of the Snagsbys' marriage. The exception to the gendering of the successful detective as male is Mrs. Bagnet, who uncovers the secret of George's identity. Significantly, she is the most masculine of the novel's women, being a "good sort of fellow herself" (393).

18. In contrast, a feminine epistemology, Dickens suggests, is at best incomplete, as the dual narration of the novel reveals. Thus Esther's perceptions may be more astute than she thinks, but her knowledge is only partial, unlike that of the omniscient narrator, whom critics universally see as male. At its worst, feminine interpretation obscures the truth. Mrs. Snagsby's efforts to detect Snagsby's "crime" create "her own dense atmosphere of dust, arising from the ceaseless working of her mill of jealousy" (737). Unlike Bucket's cloudlike atmosphere, which is both pervasive and implicitly omniscient, Mrs. Snagsby's dust is diffuse, fragmented, and, ultimately, wrong. For different perspectives on the novel's dual narration as an examination of gender characteristics, see works by Senf, who argues that the work critiques Victorian gender ideology, specifically the doctrine of "separate spheres" (1983, 21–27), and Briganti, who asserts that Esther's narrative serves as a locus for the textual unconscious,

allowing the expression of subversive states such as madness and hysteria that, associated with the feminine, have been abjected from patriarchal discourse (1990, 205–30).

19. This construction of the male reader and the (implicitly female) text confirms Laurie Langbauer's analysis of the ideological function of gender relations in Dickens. As Langbauer notes, both Dickens's presentation of women and his use of contemporary images of the mother and the hysteric stress women's submission to male power and interpretation in order to mystify and conceal men's lack of autonomy within contemporary systems of social discipline and surveillance (1990, 128–75).

Chapter 5

1. Although scholars generally agree about the movement traced by Foucault, there is some dispute about precisely when the shift took place. Alan Bray, for example, argues that the critical period is the eighteenth century (1982, 81–114), and Richard Dellamora locates the beginnings of a notion of a homosexual identity in the 1830s (1990, 1–2). Generally, however, the period from 1870 (Foucault's date) to 1890 is seen as the formative one. For a useful summary of the emergence of recognizable ideas of homosexuality in the nineteenth century, see Ed Cohen 1989. As Cohen (1989, 182–83) and Sedgwick (1985, 216–17) demonstrate, modern representations of erotic male-to-male relations were finally solidified by the public image of Wilde himself.

2. Matters are further complicated, as Sedgwick points out, by an additional set of perceptions: the simultaneous notions that homosexuality is the identity of a small number of individuals (the "minoritizing" perspective) and that both homosexual and heterosexual desires are, following the Freudian model of an innate bisexuality, inherent tendencies in everyone (the "universalizing" perspective) (1990, 84–85). Both this dichotomy and the competing definitional models of homosexuality (as inversion and as same sex object choice) persist today.

3. For a brilliant investigation of the theoretical implications of the subsequent naturalization of the homosexual/heterosexual binary, see Butler 1991.

4. See D. A. Miller's assertion (1990, 128) that the popular association of homoeroticism with anal intercourse is a reflection of castration anxiety. As Wayne Koestenbaum has demonstrated, however, the symbolics of the anus and anal intercourse can be used just as easily to deny the importance of the vagina and to erase the feminine (1989, 17–42).

5. On the most general level, the meanings of *sex* itself are restricted by the binary opposition of homosexuality and heterosexuality. The implicit definition and distinction of sexualities according to the gender of object choice excludes other possible organizations of the sexual field from consideration. For a complete discussion of this point, see Sedgwick 1990 (35, 158).

6. Traditionally, critics have been primarily concerned to restrict the scope of homosexual desire in the novel, usually attributing it almost exclusively to Basil Hallward (Nassaar 1974, 39; Shewan 1977, 113). Ellie Ragland-Sullivan (1986, 114–33) elaborates a highly sophisticated definition of homosexual desire, only

to conclude that the novel dramatizes Wilde's unconscious guilt. More recently, Ed Cohen (1987, 801–13) and Eve Sedgwick (1990, 131–81) have analyzed the novel as an attempt to articulate the emerging notion of homosexuality.

7. In fact, the depiction of Sybil in the novel implicitly asserts the fin-de-siècle idea that "woman," lacking the intellectual and spiritual capacities that constitute (male) subjectivity, exists only on the material plane (Dijkstra 1986, 219–20). Coming to console Dorian after learning of Sybil's death, Basil is shocked to find that Dorian is not deep in sorrow: "You can talk to me of other women being charming . . . before the girl you loved has even the quiet of the grave to sleep in? Why man there are horrors in store for that little white body of hers!" (112). In a novel in which the central character broods incessantly about the state of his "soul," it is curious that Basil's emphasis should fall on the body of Sybil, on the "horrors" in store for her corpse. Dorian's flippant response that Sybil never really lived and therefore is not dead serves less to contradict the assumptions behind Basil's statement than to confirm them. Only the body of Sybil can be spoken of, since Sybil in fact has no soul, no identity. If Dorian has fallen in love with the images of woman—Rosalind, Juliet, Imogen—that Sybil portrays, this is because these are in fact all Sybil is. When Lord Henry asks when she is Sybil Vane, Dorian's response is, "Never" (60). Nor is this simply the result of Sybil's vocation as an actress. As Lord Henry notes, women are a "decorative sex" who represent the "triumph of matter over mind." They are, then, simply a material plane of bodies, "sphinxes without secrets" (199), and their identities are mere fictional constructs. It is no wonder, then, that Dorian asks Basil for a sketch of Sybil so that he can remember her. Absent, Sybil must cease to exist, since she has no being beyond the material for memory to seize on. As such, Joseph's assertion (1987, 62) that Sybil represents a male figure fictionally "disguised as a woman" seems inadequate. The larger function of Sybil in the novel would seem to be to conceal, however unsuccessfully, the possibility of male objectification, precisely the function that the constitution of woman as material object serves in patriarchal culture. Thus Elaine Showalter is right to identify the novel's treatment of Sybil as misogynistic (1990, 176). This misogyny is not, however, as Showalter assumes, the inevitable, or only, implication of the fin-de-siècle argument that homosexuality, because of its (sexual) repudiation of women, is the highest refinement of increasing gender differentiation, the progressive division between male (subjects) and female (objects) mandated by evolution (Dijkstra 1986, 212–13). Although this view of homosexuality condenses patriarchal misogyny, it also inadvertently deconstructs the gendering of the subject/object binary, as the failure of Sybil to conceal the object status of the novel's male characters suggests. It is doubtless her failure to recognize the demystifying implications of same-sex object choice in this context that leads Showalter to see fin-de-siècle homosexuality not only as derived from a fear of female emancipation but also as leading to death from tuberculosis (1990, 170–71). The latter notion seems less to reveal a causal relation heretofore unsuspected by medical science than to represent a (fantasized) punishment for the homosexual's (putative) contempt for women.

8. The anxiety that can be produced by the homosexual's association with the dissolution of the self would seem to shape, metonymically, Ellmann's account of Wilde's death: "He had scarcely breathed his last breath when the body

exploded with fluids from the ear, nose, mouth, and other orifices. The debris was appalling" (1988, 584). In the context of Ellmann's larger account of the metamorphic effects of homosexuality, the emphasis here on the transformation of the (solid) body of Wilde, the material image of the unity of the self, into a variety of fluids encapsulates our cultural fears of the disintegrative effects attributed to homosexual desire.

9. Moreover, the role of connoisseur would seem to take part in what Gagnier calls the contemporary "crisis of images," in which social identities such as the dandy or the gentleman were themselves reified and marketed as commodities. As Gagnier points out, Wilde himself constructed and advertised "Oscar Wilde" as a commodity, the type of the dandy-artist (1986, 56-57). For a complete analysis of the rise of commodity culture in Victorian England, see Richards 1990 (53-72).

10. Compare Eve Sedgwick's reading (1990, 160-61) of Dorian's narcissism as a "camouflaged" expression of homoeroticism.

11. Not surprisingly, Wilde's responses to reviews of the novel duplicate the moral contradictions of the text. In a series of letters to the *Scots Observer,* Wilde alternately argues that the artist has no ethical sympathies and that *Dorian Gray* has a strong ethical lesson (1979, 82-83). The overall coherence of the work has been questioned by San Juan (1967, 52), who suggests, largely on the basis of chapter 11, that *Dorian Gray* is not a novel in the traditional sense of a series of incidents producing a single effect. See also Roditi 1969 (50). Critical attempts to impose a moral or structural unity on the work generally merely displace the text's incoherence. Thus Phillip Cohen (1978, 118-20) argues that the work contains two narrators, an amoral one who sympathizes with Dorian's behavior and a moral one who presents traditional values.

12. For a complete analysis of the emphasis on surfaces in Wilde's aesthetics, see Joseph 1987.

13. I disagree, however, with Eve Sedgwick's overall analysis of the relations between modernism and the representation of (homo)sexuality (1990, 164-67), particularly with the assertion that Wilde's evacuation of meaning in the text, which anticipates what Sedgwick calls the "empty secret" of modernism, is used to conceal the "open secret" of homosexuality.

Bibliography

Adams, Timothy Dow. 1982. "To Know the Dancer from the Dance: Dance as Metaphor of Marriage in Four Novels of Jane Austen." *Studies in the Novel* 14:55–65.

Allen, Dennis. 1985. "No Love for Lydia: The Fate of Desire in *Pride and Prejudice.*" *TSLL* 27:425–43.

Armstrong, Nancy. 1987. *Desire and Domestic Fiction: A Political History of the Novel.* New York: Oxford University Press.

Auerbach, Nina. 1978. *Communities of Women.* Cambridge: Harvard University Press.

———. 1982. *Woman and the Demon: The Life of a Victorian Myth.* Cambridge: Harvard University Press.

Austen, Jane. [1813] 1932. *Pride and Prejudice. The Novels of Jane Austen.* Vol. 2. Ed. R. W. Chapman. 3d ed. London: Oxford University Press.

Babb, Howard. 1962. *Jane Austen's Novels: The Fabric of Dialogue.* Columbus: Ohio State University Press.

Barthes, Roland. 1972. *Mythologies.* Trans. Annette Lavers. New York: Hill and Wang.

———. 1974. *S/Z.* Trans. Richard Miller. New York: Hill and Wang.

———. 1975. *The Pleasure of the Text.* Trans. Richard Miller. New York: Hill and Wang.

Baudrillard, Jean. 1981. *For a Critique of the Political Economy of the Sign.* Trans. Charles Levin. St. Louis: Telos.

Beer, Gillian. 1983. *Darwin's Plots: Evolutionary Narrative in Darwin, George Eliot, and Nineteenth-Century Fiction.* London: Routledge.

Benjamin, Walter. [1955] 1986. "Paris, Capital of the Nineteenth Century." In *Reflections,* ed. Peter Demetz, 146–62. New York: Schocken.

Bernheimer, Charles, and Claire Kahane, eds. 1985. *In Dora's Case: Freud—Hysteria—Feminism.* New York: Columbia University Press.

Bersani, Leo. 1986. *The Freudian Body: Psychoanalysis and Art.* New York: Columbia University Press.

Bibliography

Birken, Lawrence. 1988. *Consuming Desire: Sexual Science and the Emergence of a Culture of Abundance, 1871–1914*. Ithaca: Cornell University Press.

Blain, Virginia. 1985. "Double Vision and the Double Standard in *Bleak House:* A Feminist Perspective." *Literature and History* 11:31–46.

Bonaparte, Marie. 1935. "The Murders in the Rue Morgue." *Psychoanalytic Quarterly* 4:259–93.

Boone, Joseph Allen. 1987. *Tradition Counter Tradition: Love and the Form of Fiction*. Chicago: University of Chicago Press.

Brantlinger, Patrick. 1988. *Rule of Darkness: British Literature and Imperialism, 1830–1914*. Ithaca: Cornell University Press.

Bray, Alan. 1982. *Homosexuality in Renaissance England*. London: Gay Men's Press.

Briganti, Chiara. 1990. "The Monstrous Actress: Esther Summerson's Spectral Name." *Dickens Studies Annual* 19:205–30.

Brontë, Charlotte. [1847] 1960. *Jane Eyre*. New York: Signet.

———. [1850] 1968. Letter to W. S. Williams, 12 April. Reprint. In *Jane Austen: The Critical Heritage,* ed. B. C. Southam, 128. London: Routledge.

Butler, Judith. 1990. *Gender Trouble: Feminism and the Subversion of Identity*. New York: Routledge.

———. "Imitation and Gender Insubordination." In *Inside/Out: Lesbian Theories, Gay Theories,* ed. Diana Fuss, 13–31. New York: Routledge.

Butler, Marilyn. 1975. *Jane Austen and the War of Ideas*. Oxford: Clarendon Press.

Cannon, Walter F. 1968. "Darwin's Vision in *On the Origin of Species.*" In *The Art of Victorian Prose,* ed. George Levine and William Madden, 154–76. New York: Oxford University Press.

Carpenter, Edward. 1897. *Civilisation: Its Cause and Cure and Other Essays*. 5th ed. London: Swan Sonnenschein.

Castle, Terry. 1986. *Masquerade and Civilization*. Stanford: Stanford University Press.

Chandler, Alice. 1975. " 'A Pair of Fine Eyes': Jane Austen's Treatment of Sex." *Studies in the Novel* 7:88–103.

Chodorow, Nancy. 1987. *The Reproduction of Mothering: Psychoanalysis and the Sociology of Gender*. Berkeley: University of California Press.

Cohen, Ed. 1987. "Writing Gone Wilde: Homoerotic Desire in the Closet of Representation." *PMLA* 102:801–13.

———. 1989. "Legislating the Norm: From Sodomy to Gross Indecency." *SAQ* 88:181–217.

Cohen, Phillip. 1978. *The Moral Vision of Oscar Wilde*. Rutherford, N.J.: Fairleigh Dickinson University Press.

Craft, Christopher. 1990. "Alias Bunbury: Desire and Termination in *The Importance of Being Earnest.*" *Representations* 31:19–46.

Darwin, Charles. [1859] 1985. *The Origin of Species by Means of Natural Selection; or, The Preservation of Favoured Races in the Struggle for Life*. Ed. J. W. Burrow. New York: Penguin.

David, Deirdre. N.d. "The War on Thuggee: The Battle for Knowledge." Unpublished paper.

Davis, Robert Con. 1983. "Lacan, Poe, and Narrative Repression." In *Lacan*

Bibliography

and Narration, ed. Robert Con Davis, 983–1005. Baltimore: Johns Hopkins University Press.

Dellamora, Richard. 1990. *Masculine Desire: The Sexual Politics of Victorian Aestheticism.* Chapel Hill: University of North Carolina Press.

de Rougemont, Denis. [1956] 1974. *Love in the Western World.* New York: Pantheon.

Dickens, Charles. [1852–53] 1964. *Bleak House.* New York: Signet.

Dijkstra, Bram. 1986. *Idols of Perversity: Fantasies of Feminine Evil in Fin-de-Siècle Culture.* New York: Oxford University Press.

Dodsworth, Martin. 1963. "Women without Men at Cranford." *Essays in Criticism* 13:132–45.

Dollimore, Jonathan. 1991. *Sexual Dissidence: Augustine to Wilde, Freud to Foucault.* Oxford: Clarendon Press.

Doyle, Sir Arthur Conan. [1902] 1963. *The Hound of the Baskervilles.* New York: Berkley.

Duckworth, Alistair. 1971. *The Improvement of the Estate.* Baltimore: Johns Hopkins University Press.

Ellmann, Richard. 1988. *Oscar Wilde.* New York: Knopf.

Elsbree, Langdon. 1960. "Jane Austen and the Dance of Fidelity and Complaisance." *Nineteenth-Century Fiction* 15:113–36.

Felman, Shoshana. 1981. "Rereading Femininity." *Yale French Studies* 62:19–44.

Fergus, Jan S. 1981. "Sex and Social Life in Jane Austen's Novels." In *Jane Austen in a Social Context,* ed. David Monaghan, 66–85. London: Macmillan.

Foucault, Michel. 1978. *The History of Sexuality: An Introduction.* Trans. Robert Hurley. New York: Pantheon.

Fowler, Rowena. 1984. "*Cranford:* Cow in Grey Flannel or Lion Couchant?" *SEL* 24:717–29.

Frank, Lawrence. 1984. *Charles Dickens and the Romantic Self.* Lincoln: University of Nebraska Press.

Freud, Sigmund. [1905] 1961. *Fragment of an Analysis of a Case of Hysteria.* In *The Standard Edition of the Complete Psychological Works of Sigmund Freud,* ed. and trans. James Strachey, 7:7–122. London: Hogarth Press.

———. [1909] 1961. "Some General Remarks on Hysterical Attacks." In *The Standard Edition of the Complete Psychological Works of Sigmund Freud,* ed. and trans. James Strachey, 9:227–34. London: Hogarth Press.

———. [1930] 1961. *Civilization and Its Discontents.* In *The Standard Edition of the Complete Psychological Works of Sigmund Freud,* ed. and trans. James Strachey, 21:64–148. London: Hogarth Press.

Fuss, Diana. 1989. *Essentially Speaking: Feminism, Nature, and Difference.* New York: Routledge.

Gagnier, Regenia. 1986. *Idylls of the Marketplace: Oscar Wilde and the Victorian Public.* Stanford: Stanford University Press.

———. 1991. *Subjectivities: A History of Self-Representation in Britain, 1832–1920.* New York: Oxford University Press.

Gallagher, Catherine. 1987. "The Body versus the Social Body in the Works of Thomas Malthus and Henry Mayhew." In *The Making of the Modern Body: Sexuality and Society in the Nineteenth Century,* ed. Catherine Gallagher and Thomas Laqueur, 83–106. Berkeley: University of California Press.

Bibliography

Gallop, Jane. 1982. *The Daughter's Seduction: Feminism and Psychoanalysis.* Ithaca: Cornell University Press.

Garber, Marjorie. 1992. *Vested Interests: Cross-Dressing and Cultural Anxiety.* New York: Routledge.

Gaskell, Elizabeth. [1851–53] 1976. *Cranford.* Ed. Peter Keating. New York: Penguin.

Gay, Peter. 1984. *The Education of the Senses.* Vol. 1 of *The Bourgeois Experience: Victoria to Freud.* New York: Oxford University Press.

———. 1986. *The Tender Passion.* Vol. 2 of *The Bourgeois Experience: Victoria to Freud.* New York: Oxford University Press.

Geertz, Clifford. 1973. *The Interpretation of Cultures.* New York: Basic Books.

Gide, André. [1949] 1969. "In Memoriam." In *Oscar Wilde: A Collection of Critical Essays,* ed. Richard Ellmann, 25–34. Englewood Cliffs, N.J.: Prentice-Hall.

Gilbert, Sandra, and Susan Gubar. 1979. *The Madwoman in the Attic.* New Haven: Yale University Press.

Gilman, Sander. 1985. *Difference and Pathology: Stereotypes of Sexuality, Race, and Madness.* Ithaca: Cornell University Press.

Goldfarb, Russell. 1970. *Sexual Repression and Victorian Literature.* Lewisburg, Pa.: Bucknell University Press.

Hardy, Thomas. [1891] 1978. *Tess of the d'Urbervilles: A Pure Woman.* Ed. David Skilton. New York: Penguin.

Hawthorne, Julian. [1890] 1970. "The Romance of the Impossible." *Lippincott's* 46:412–15. Reprint. In *Oscar Wilde: The Critical Heritage,* ed. Karl Beckson, 79–80. New York: Barnes and Noble.

Heath, Stephen. 1984. *The Sexual Fix.* New York: Schocken.

Heilman, Robert B. 1975. "*E pluribus unum:* Parts and Whole in *Pride and Prejudice.*" In *Jane Austen: Bicentenary Essays,* ed. John Halperin, 123–43. Cambridge: Cambridge University Press.

Hertz, Neil. 1985. "Dora's Secrets, Freud's Techniques." In *In Dora's Case: Freud—Hysteria—Feminism,* ed. Charles Bernheimer and Claire Kahane, 221–42. New York: Columbia University Press.

Hocquenghem, Guy. 1978. *Homosexual Desire.* Trans. Daniella Dangoor. London: Allison and Busby.

Homans, Margaret. 1986. *Bearing the Word: Language and Female Experience in Nineteenth-Century Women's Writing.* Chicago: University of Chicago Press.

Houghton, Walter. 1957. *The Victorian Frame of Mind: 1830–1870.* New Haven: Yale University Press.

Hutter, Albert D. 1983. "The Novelist as Resurrectionist: Dickens and the Dilemma of Death." *Dickens Studies Annual* 12:1–39.

Irigaray, Luce. 1985. *This Sex Which Is Not One.* Trans. Catherine Porter with Carolyn Burke. Ithaca: Cornell University Press.

Jacobus, Mary. 1986. *Reading Woman: Essays in Feminist Criticism.* New York: Columbia University Press.

Jameson, Fredric. 1981. *The Political Unconscious: Narrative as a Socially Symbolic Act.* Ithaca: Cornell University Press.

Bibliography

Johnson, Claudia. 1988. *Jane Austen: Women, Politics, and the Novel*. Chicago: University of Chicago Press.

Johnson, Wendell Stacy. 1975. *Sex and Marriage in Victorian Poetry*. Ithaca: Cornell University Press.

Joseph, Gerhard. 1987. "Framing Wilde." *Victorian Newsletter* 72:61-63.

Kaplan, Deborah. 1992. *Jane Austen among Women*. Baltimore: Johns Hopkins University Press.

Kincaid, James R. 1987. "Viewing and Blurring in Dickens: The Misrepresentation of Representation." *Dickens Studies Annual* 16:95-111.

Koestenbaum, Wayne. 1989. *Double Talk: The Erotics of Male Literary Collaboration*. New York: Routledge.

Krasner, James. 1990. "A Chaos of Delight: Perception and Illusion in Darwin's Scientific Writing." *Representations* 31:118-41.

Kristeva, Julia. 1986. "Stabat Mater." In *The Female Body in Western Culture*, ed. Susan Rubin Suleiman, 99-118. Cambridge: Harvard University Press.

Kucich, John. 1981. *Excess and Restraint in the Novels of Charles Dickens*. Athens: University of Georgia Press.

———. 1987. *Repression in Victorian Fiction: Charlotte Brontë, George Eliot, and Charles Dickens*. Berkeley: University of California Press.

Langbauer, Laurie. 1990. *Women and Romance: The Consolations of Gender in the English Novel*. Ithaca: Cornell University Press.

Laqueur, Thomas. 1990. *Making Sex: Body and Gender from the Greeks to Freud*. Cambridge: Harvard University Press.

Lukacher, Ned. 1986. *Primal Scenes: Literature, Philosophy, Psychoanalysis*. Ithaca: Cornell University Press.

McMaster, Juliet. 1978. *Jane Austen on Love*. ELS Monograph Series, no. 13. Victoria: University of Victoria Press.

Malone, Cynthia Northcutt. 1990. " 'Flight' and 'Pursuit': Fugitive Identity in *Bleak House*." *Dickens Studies Annual* 19:107-24.

Mansell, Darrell. 1973. *The Novels of Jane Austen: An Interpretation*. New York: Macmillan.

Marcus, Stephen. [1966] 1985. *The Other Victorians: A Study of Sexuality and Pornography in Mid-Nineteenth-Century England*. Reprint. New York: Norton.

Mayhew, Henry. [1862] 1968. *London Labour and the London Poor*. Vol. 4. London: Griffin, Bohn. Reprint. New York: Dover.

Michie, Helena. 1987. *The Flesh Made Word: Female Figures and Women's Bodies*. New York: Oxford University Press.

———. 1989. " 'Who is this in Pain?': Scarring, Disfigurement, and Female Identity in *Bleak House* and *Our Mutual Friend*." *Novel* 22:199-212.

Miller, D. A. 1981. *Narrative and Its Discontents: Problems of Closure in the Traditional Novel*. Princeton: Princeton University Press.

———. 1988. *The Novel and the Police*. Berkeley: University of California Press.

———. 1990. "Anal *Rope*." *Representations* 32:114-33.

Moi, Toril. 1985. "Representation of Patriarchy: Sexuality and Epistemology in Freud's Dora." In *In Dora's Case: Freud—Hysteria—Feminism,* ed. Charles

Bibliography

Bernheimer and Claire Kahane, 181–99. New York: Columbia University Press.

"Moore's Epistles, Odes, and other Poems." 1806. *Eclectic Review* 2, pt. 2:811–15.

Morgan, Susan. 1980. *In the Meantime: Character and Perception in Jane Austen's Fiction.* Chicago: University of Chicago Press.

———. 1989. *Sisters in Time: Imagining Gender in Nineteenth-Century British Fiction.* New York: Oxford University Press.

Mudrick, Marvin. 1952. *Jane Austen: Irony as Defense and Discovery.* Princeton: Princeton University Press.

Nardin, Jane. 1973. *Those Elegant Decorums.* Albany: State University of New York Press.

Nassaar, Christopher. 1974. *Into the Demon Universe.* New Haven: Yale University Press.

Pearsall, Ronald. 1969. *The Worm in the Bud: The World of Victorian Sexuality.* Toronto: Macmillan.

Polhemus, Robert M. 1990. *Erotic Faith: Being in Love from Jane Austen to D. H. Lawrence.* Chicago: University of Chicago Press.

Poovey, Mary. 1984. *The Proper Lady and the Woman Writer: Ideology as Style in the Works of Mary Wollstonecraft, Mary Shelley, and Jane Austen.* Chicago: University of Chicago Press.

———. 1988. *Uneven Developments: The Ideological Work of Gender in Mid-Victorian England.* Chicago: University of Chicago Press.

Ragland-Sullivan, Ellie. 1986. "The Phenomenon of Aging in Oscar Wilde's *Picture of Dorian Gray:* A Lacanian View." In *Memory and Desire: Aging—Literature—Psychoanalysis,* ed. Kathleen Woodward and Murray Schwartz, 1114–33. Bloomington: Indiana University Press.

Reade, W. Winwood. 1863. *Savage Africa.* London: Smith, Elder.

Richards, Thomas. 1990. *The Commodity Culture of Victorian England: Advertising and Spectacle, 1851–1914.* Stanford: Stanford University Press.

Rieff, Philip. 1963. "Introduction." In *Dora: An Analysis of a Case of Hysteria,* by Sigmund Freud, 7–20. New York: Collier.

Roditi, Edouard. 1969. "Fiction as Allegory: *The Picture of Dorian Gray.*" In *Oscar Wilde: A Collection of Critical Essays,* ed. Richard Ellmann, 47–55. Englewood Cliffs, N.J.: Prentice-Hall.

Rose, Jacqueline. 1986. *Sexuality in the Field of Vision.* London: Verso.

Ruskin, John. [1880] 1963. "Fiction Fair and Foul: Essay 1." In *The Genius of John Ruskin: A Selection of His Writings,* ed. John D. Rosenberg, 435–44. Boston: Riverside.

Russett, Cynthia. 1989. *Sexual Science: The Victorian Construction of Womanhood.* Cambridge: Harvard University Press.

Sadoff, Dianne. 1982. *Monsters of Affection: Dickens, Eliot, and Brontë on Fatherhood.* Baltimore: Johns Hopkins University Press.

San Juan, Epifanio. 1967. *The Art of Oscar Wilde.* Princeton: Princeton University Press.

Schor, Hilary. 1989. "Affairs of the Alphabet: Reading, Writing, and Narrating in *Cranford.*" *Novel* 22:288–304.

Sedgwick, Eve Kosofsky. 1985. *Between Men: English Literature and Male Homosocial Desire.* New York: Columbia University Press.

Bibliography

————. 1990. *Epistemology of the Closet.* Berkeley: University of California Press.

Senf, Carol A. 1983. "*Bleak House:* Dickens, Esther, and the Androgynous Mind." *Victorian Newsletter* 64:21–27.

Shewan, Rodney. 1977. *Oscar Wilde: Art and Egotism.* New York: Barnes and Noble.

Showalter, Elaine. 1981. "Feminist Criticism in the Wilderness." *Critical Inquiry* 8:179–205.

————. 1990. *Sexual Anarchy: Gender and Culture at the Fin de Siècle.* New York: Viking.

Sinha, Mrinalini. 1987. "Gender and Imperialism: Colonial Policy and the Ideology of Moral Imperialism in Late Nineteenth-Century Bengal." In *Changing Men: New Directions in Research on Men and Masculinity,* ed. Michael S. Kimmel, 217–31. Newbury Park, Calif.: Sage.

Smith, Leroy. 1983. *Jane Austen and the Drama of Woman.* New York: St. Martin's Press.

Spacks, Patricia Meyer. 1990. *Desire and Truth: Functions of Plot in Eighteenth-Century English Novels.* Chicago: University of Chicago Press.

Sprengnether, Madelon. 1985. "Enforcing Oedipus: Freud and Dora." In *The (M)other Tongue: Essays in Feminist Psychoanalytic Interpretation,* ed. Shirley Nelson Garner, Claire Kahane, and Madelon Sprengnether, 51–71. Ithaca: Cornell University Press.

Spivak, Gayatri. 1986. "Imperialism and Sexual Difference." *Oxford Literary Review* 8:225–40.

Stewart, Garrett. 1978. "The New Mortality of *Bleak House.*" *ELH* 45:443–87.

————. 1984. *Death Sentences: Styles of Dying in British Fiction.* Cambridge: Harvard University Press.

Stone, Lawrence. 1977. *The Family, Sex, and Marriage in England, 1500–1800.* New York: Harper and Row.

Sulloway, Alison. 1989. *Jane Austen and the Province of Womanhood.* Philadelphia: University of Pennsylvania Press.

Tanner, Tony. 1986. *Jane Austen.* Cambridge: Harvard University Press.

Thackeray, William Makepeace. [1847–48] 1963. *Vanity Fair.* Ed. Geoffrey Tillotson and Kathleen Tillotson. Boston: Riverside.

Thompson, James. 1988. *Between Self and World: The Novels of Jane Austen.* University Park: Pennsylvania State University Press.

Trudgill, Eric. 1976. *Madonnas and Magdalens: The Origin and Development of Victorian Sexual Attitudes.* New York: Holmes and Meier.

van Boheemen, Christine. 1987. *The Novel as Family Romance: Language, Gender, and Authority from Fielding to Joyce.* Ithaca: Cornell University Press.

Weeks, Jeffrey. 1977. *Coming Out: Homosexual Politics in Britain from the Nineteenth Century to the Present.* London: Quartet.

————. 1981. *Sex, Politics, and Society: The Regulation of Sexuality since 1800.* London: Longman.

Weinstein, Philip M. 1984. *The Semantics of Desire: Changing Models of Identity from Dickens to Joyce.* Princeton: Princeton University Press.

Welsh, Alexander. 1971. *The City of Dickens.* Oxford: Clarendon Press.

Bibliography

Whibley, Charles. [1890] 1970. "Reviews and Magazines." *Scots Observer,* 5 July, 118. Reprint. In *Oscar Wilde: The Critical Heritage,* ed. Karl Beckson, 75. New York: Barnes and Noble.

Wilde, Oscar. [1891] 1968. *The Picture of Dorian Gray.* New York: Dell.

————. 1979. *Selected Letters of Oscar Wilde.* Ed. Rupert Hart-Davis. Oxford: Oxford University Press.

Williams, Raymond. 1976. *Keywords: A Vocabulary of Culture and Society.* New York: Oxford University Press.

Willis, Lesley H. 1976. "Eyes and the Imagery of Sight in *Pride and Prejudice.*" *English Studies in Canada* 2:156–62.

Wolfe, Patricia. 1968. "Structure and Movement in *Cranford.*" *Nineteenth-Century Fiction* 23:161–76.

Zwerdling, Alex. 1973. "Esther Summerson Rehabilitated." *PMLA* 88:429–39.

Index

Index

Index

Index

Representation: and containment of the body, 84, 92–97, 99–100; of death, 85; Dickens's manipulation of, 109; of sexuality, 46, 51–57, 71, 80–81, 112; sexuality of, 83; silence as a form of, 3–4, 86

Repression: construction of, 45–51, 57–58, 109; as containment, 50; of desire, 48, 64; rejection of, 134–36. *See also* Sexual repression

Rieff, Philip, 101

Ross, Robert, 110, 112

Ruskin, John, 90–91

Russett, Cynthia, 25, 75

Satisfaction, 45–51; and ascesis, 47–48

Scopic economy, 117–20, 128

Sedgwick, Eve, 113, 120, 134

Self: destabilised by sexuality, 90–91, 117, 123; regulation of, 9; reification of, 127

Sex: defined, 5–7, 36; erasure of, 66, 103; and reproduction, 62–64, 74, 78

Sexual: appetite, 63; cultural representations of the, 37, 70–77, 80–82; internalization of the, 49; regulation of the, 63; troping of the, 38–45

Sexual desire: articulation of, 46, 49–50, 57; Austen and, 31, 41–48; defined, 43; Dickens and, 86, 97–98; Gaskell and, 62–64; infinite substitutability of, 44, 47, 50; prudery in nineteenth-century depictions of, 3, 27; regulation of, 42, 45, 50, 70; Wilde and, 110–36

Sexuality: as chaotic, 8, 13–14, 18, 22, 38–41, 56–57, 113–15; and guilt, 89; and homosexuality, 112; and indifferent, 42, 44, 115; indirect representation of, 52–57, 80–82, 134; of knowledge, 104–109; as a locus of undecidability, 98; mystery of,

84, 98, 101–109; nineteenth-century recodification of, 113; production and containment of, 4, 35, 52, 54, 56; resistance to representation of, 32, 34, & n, 35, 38, 45, 98–99, 116, 134; and somatic disruption, 38–40; Victorian reticence about, 30–39, 51, 61–83; and violence, 39–41. *See also* Homosexuality, Sex, Sexual desire

Sexual repression, 48–51, 65–66, 86, 88–90; as class indicator, 69–70; as constitutive of narrative, 58, 86; defined, 38

Showalter, Elaine, 60, 130–31

Social class: sexuality and, 21, 26–28, 42; Victorian views of, 26, 64, 66

Social Darwinism, 25. *See also* Darwin, Charles

Social order, and distinctions, 41, 42, 54

Spivak, Gayatri Chakravorty, 94

Stewart, Garrett, 85

Subjectivity, 49n.7; inter-, 106; in Wilde, 116–19, 125

Tanner, Tony, 52

Taxonomy, 21–28, 34–35, 129; instability of gender categories, 72–73; social, 28n, 64, 69

Tess of the d'Urbervilles, 3–4; exclusion of sexuality in, 43–46

Text: as body, 97–109; body as, 92–97; hysteric body as, 102, 104

Textualization. *See* Narrativization

Thackeray, William Makepeace. See *Vanity Fair*

Vanity Fair, 20, 31–32

Victorian: ideas of gender, 61–62; ideas of sex and sexuality, 4 & n.1, 5, 9, 70, 109, 115; ideology, 16–17; notions of genetics, 123–24; read-

160